AIR FRYER COOKBOOK MASTERY

90 Unbelievably Delicious Recipes and Cooking Guide to Step Up Your Air Frying Game

JEREMY HORNER

CONTENTS

Part One
WELCOME TO THE WORLD OF AIR FRYERS

1. What Are Air Fryers? — 3
2. How Do They Work? — 4
3. What Are The Types Of Air Fryers? — 5
4. What Are Their Most Useful Features? — 8
5. What Are The Benefits Of Using Them? — 11
6. What Are The Most Important Things to Remember About Their Use? — 15

Part Two
BREAKFAST RECIPES

Cheesy and Peppery Vegetable Omelet	23
Tomato and Spinach Scrambled Eggs	24
Easy Egg Breakfast	25
Toasties and Sausage Surprise	27
Parsley and Spinach Baked Omelet	29
Easy-peasy Cheesy Omelet	30
Brazilian Turkey Pies	31
Easy-peasy English-style Breakfast	33
Sloppy Joe Stuffed Scones	35
Apricot and French Toast Delight	37
Zucchini and Carrot Muffins	39
Pecan and Pumpkin Muffins	41
Savory Corn and Scallion Cakes	43
Fast Breakfast Shrimp Toasts	45
Carrot, Cucumber and Salmon Mix	46
Basic Breakfast Donuts	47
Spicy Chicken, Vegetables, and Shell Spaghetti Special	49
Vegan Taco Crisp Wraps	51
Easy Vegetable Pasta Salad with Balsamic Vinegar Dressing	52
Italian Chicken-flavored Cheesy Risotto	54
Kid-friendly Spinach Balls	56
Potato Bread Rolls	57

Cheesy Potato Wedges	59
Homemade Vegetable Pizza on Toast	60
Yummy Maple Cinnamon Buns	61
Cheesy Vegetable Breakfast Frittata	63
Quick Cheddar and Bacon Quiche	65
Sumptuous Beginner's Soufflé	67
Banana Cinnamon Bread	69
Liver Pate	70

Part Three
LUNCH AND DINNER RECIPES

Black Cod with Grapes and Pecan Toppings	73
Colorful Pasta Salad with Roasted Vegetables	75
Philly Chicken Cheesesteak Stromboli	77
Inside Out Cheeseburgers	79
Chinese-style Roasted Cauliflower with General Tso Sauce	81
Sockeye Salmon en Papillotte	83
Garlic and Parmesan Shrimp	85
Stuffed Chicken with Pizza Filling	87
Mac and Cheese	89
Classic Steak and Roasted Potatoes	91
Air Fryer-style Vegetable Galore	93
Crispy Fried Chicken with Roasted Veggies	95
Gluten-Free Salmon Croquettes	97
Classic Roast Chicken	98
Chinese Sweet and Sour Pork	100
Kabab Koobideh	102
Cheesy Chicken Parmesan	104
Tijuana-style Street Taco	106
Crispy Noodle Salad	108
Flourless Chicken Cordon Bleu	110
Roasted Stuffed Peppers	112
Turkey Breast with Maple Mustard Glaze	114
Crispy Roast Pork	116
Sticky Mushroom Rice	118
Cajun-style Salmon	120
Bang Bang Fried Shrimp	121
Baked Garlic Parsley Potatoes	123
Salt and Pepper Pork Chops	124
Ravioli with Marinara Sauce	126
Mushroom Chicken Broccoli Casserole	127

Part Four
DESSERT RECIPES

Mini Strawberry Rolls	131
Apple Dumplings	133
Chocolate Chip Cookies	135
Nutella Banana Sandwich	137
Fruit Crumble Mug Cakes	139
Blondie and Brownie Bars	141
Banana-Vanilla Pastry Puffs	143
Easy Chocolate Soufflés	145
S'mores in a Banana Treat	147
Single Serve Chocolate Mug Cake	149
Apple Fries with Caramel Cream Dip	150
Ricotta and Lemon Cheesecake	152
Merry Berry Pavlova	153
Pineapple, Honey and Coconut Delight	155
Crème Brûlée	156
Lemon Butter Pound Cake	158
Coconut Banana Treat	160
Hazelnut Brownie Cups	162
Tarte Tatin	164
Butter and Marshmallow Fluff Turnovers	166
Cherry Clafoutis	168
Apricot and Blackberry Crumble	170
Pear and Apple Crisp with Walnuts	172
Pear Parcels	174
Chocolate Lava Cake	176
Tangy Orange Carrot Cake	178
Easy Chocolate Éclairs with a Flair	180
Salty Pistachio Brownies	182
Chocolate Brownies with Caramel Sauce	184
White Chocolate and Almond Cookies	186

Copyright © 2018

All rights reserved.

The information provided herein is stated to be truthful and consistent, in that any liability, in terms of inattention or otherwise, by any usage or abuse of any policies, processes, or directions contained within is the solitary and utter responsibility of the recipient reader. Under no circumstances will any legal responsibility or blame be held against the publisher for any reparation, damages, or monetary loss due to the information herein, either directly or indirectly.

This book has been written purely for informational and educational purposes. The presentation of the information is without contract or any type of guarantee assurance.

The trademarks that are used are without any consent, and the publication of the trademark is without permission or backing by the trademark owner. All trademarks and brands within this article are for clarifying purposes only and are the owned by the owners themselves, not affiliated with this document.

Part One

WELCOME TO THE WORLD OF AIR FRYERS

Buy an air fryer now and start your journey toward a healthy diet and lifestyle! The claim seems absurd because it isn't the cooking equipment per se but the cooking technique that makes for healthier dishes and desserts.

But when you consider the benefits of using an air fryer for grilling, baking and frying your food, you immediately realize that, indeed, there's more than a grain of truth in the claim. The fact that less oil is necessary is one of the reasons for its increasing popularity among health-conscious individuals, from athletes to college students.

But don't take our word for it! The proof of the pudding is in the eating so you should buy an air fryer and put it to the test.

In the following sections, I will share everything you need to know about air fryers – what these are, how to use them well, and what dishes and desserts you can make using them, among others. Read on not only because you paid for the book – and I want to thank you for purchasing it and I hope that you will find good uses for it – but because the information contained here will be truly useful in your life!

Also included is 30 recipes – 30 each for three sections, namely, breakfast, lunch and dinner, and desserts – so that you can use your air fryer for a month and see what it can do in relation to your healthy lifestyle. You can, of course, mix and match these recipes for the succeeding months, as well as make your own creations by substituting ingredients.

Chapter One

WHAT ARE AIR FRYERS?

The first air fryers were introduced in Australia and Europe in 2010 so these are relatively new kitchen appliances. Due to their numerous benefits and uses, however, their popularity is on the rise in the United States, Canada, and Japan as well as in India.

While these can be used for a wide range of cooking purposes, many countries seem to have favorite uses for them. For example, the Dutch and British like using them for chips, the Japanese for fried prawns, and the Americans for chicken wings.

By definition, air fryers are kitchen appliances that cook meats, vegetables and herbs, among other ingredients, via the circulation of hot air around them. These typically have mechanical fans that circulate the hot air at high speed, which simultaneously cooks the food and creates a crispy layer.

Known as the Maillard effect, the juicy-on-the-inside, crispy-on-the-outside cooking effect can be achieved via the traditional means by complete submersion of the food in hot oil – or deep frying, as we call it. In contrast, air frying requires only a thin layer of oil, usually a tablespoon or two depending on the amount of food, coating the food while the hot air makes the Maillard effect possible.

At first glance, air fryers look like a cross between rice cookers and convection ovens. These come in several colors, too, from the sleek black air fryers to the sophisticated red ones. The choice in color is a personal preference while the choice in features, such as the cooking capacity, temperature adjustment, and cook time are largely influenced by the intended uses for an air fryer.

Chapter Two

HOW DO THEY WORK?

Air fryers work in many ways like convection ovens although the former are typically smaller than the latter, as well as generate less heat. So, if you have used a convection oven before, you will appreciate the way an air fryer works.

Air fryers use rapid air technology wherein hot air is circulated within the interior compartment so that the food can be cooked, which can either be grilled, baked or roasted depending on the time and temperature settings. The heating element in an air fryer's cooking chamber creates and radiates the heat while the mechanical fan circulates it.

The temperature can range from 100°F to 400°F. At these temperatures, the air fryer can be used to cook a wide range of foods from fish, chicken and meat to vegetables and pastries with significantly less oil than in traditional deep frying. These temperatures also demand that safety precautions be applied, such as no placing of oil inside the cooking chamber and no placing of flammable objects near it.

The opening of the top in a typical air fryer is necessary for taking air in so don't cover it, if it's in the design. In many models, there's an exhaust at the back that serves two purposes, namely, to release excess hot air resulting in better temperature control and to prevent undesirable increase in internal pressure. The bottom line: Never tamper with the design of an air fryer because there are safety reasons for its features, both inside and out.

Chapter Three
WHAT ARE THE TYPES OF AIR FRYERS?

These must-have kitchen appliances come in several types so there will always be one model that meets every individual's needs in it. Before browsing your choices, however, you are well-advised to consider your budget, your planned uses for it, and your desired features. These factors will influence your final choice, especially when you have dozens of choices available.

Let's first look at the way that air fryers operate, which can be either analog or digital. Analog air fryers typically have knobs and/or switches for their operations, from turning on and off the unit to adjusting the time and temperature settings. These are typically more affordable than their digital counterparts but not necessarily less efficient or designed with less features.

Digital air fryers typically have touchscreen display panels where the temperature and time settings can be adjusted; the power switch may be a button or a part of the touchscreen panel. These have more modern designs than the analog air fryers, as well as more intuitive (i.e., user-friendly) especially for people with smart devices (e.g., digital kitchen appliances and smartphones). These also come with more and better options than traditional air fryers but these come at a price.

The choice between an analog and a digital air fryer boils down to your personal preferences. Each one can be as efficient as the other with proper use, a matter that we will discuss in a succeeding section.

Air fryers are also classified according to the cooking approach with the major types being the following.

PADDLE AIR FRYERS

These are the first type of air fryers to be introduced into the consumer market and, thus, are the most familiar to users. The typical paddle air fryer has a saucer-shaped design with a detachable bowl, lid and paddle.

Due to their deep design, these can be used for cooking foods with liquids, such as sauces; examples include curry and risotto. Since there's a paddle included, there's no need to turn the food at regular intervals during the cooking process. You just place the food into the cooking chamber, set the timer and temperature, and let the air fryer do the work.

Keep in mind that a paddle air fryer can be used with or without its paddle. You can use the paddle for stirring food, if necessary, or not use it when you cooking delicate food; the paddle can sometimes smash the food so its texture and consistency changes.

BASKET AIR FRYERS

These cook food inside a basket, an easy approach that beginners appreciate. You just place the food for frying inside the basket, place both in the air fryer, and set the time and temperature before turning on the appliance.

Basket air fryers are great for foods that have been battered or coated, such as chicken wings and onion rings. These can also be used for cooking two different foods at the same time due to the divider feature. These also have basket housing for catching food and oil residues, such as grease, as well as a dishwasher-friendly basket.

Be sure to toss the food at regular intervals while it's cooking. Otherwise, you will end up with partially cooked food.

Due to their compact size, these are popular among college students, owners of recreational vehicles, and tenants in studio apartments, among other people living in modest accommodations. Many people even use them in outdoor situations, such as in picnics and glamping.

OVEN AIR FRYERS

These are more versatile than the basket air fryers because these can broil, grill, bake, roast, and steam, even dehydrate, food. In fact, these can be used for toasting bread, roasting coffee, and roasting chicken, sometimes cooking two types of food at a time.

But you shouldn't pile up the food in an oven air fryer's cooking chamber if you want even cooking results. You will find that it's suitable for cooking in smaller portions, aside from the need for regular turning of the food while cooking.

While an oven air fryer will not heat up your kitchen like a regular oven, its glass cooking bowl can become extremely hot during the cooking process. You may also find it heavier and, thus, more cumbersome than many of the other types of air fryers.

INFRARED HALOGEN AIR FRYERS

These are extremely efficient air fryers because of their use of infrared rays in cooking; the rays are created by halogen lights. The food can become cooked faster in comparison with tother types, aside from the fact that infrared halogen air fryers can be used for a wide variety of cooking methods. These can also handle most types of food.

Infrared halogen air fryers are equipped with a thermostat for safe and effective temperature regulation. The thermostat is part of a mechanism that turns the halogen bulb on and off, as necessary.

But these air fryers aren't as popular as the paddle, basket and oven air fryers. These often have shorter lifespans, mainly due to the halogen bulb burning out quickly; the bulb itself can be difficult and expensive to replace so much so that it's often better to buy a new unit.

Which of these types is the best? Well, it depends on your specific needs and wants. You will benefit from an oven air fryer if you're looking for a multipurpose unit, while a basket air fryer may be your best choice if you're planning on just frying food with it.

Chapter Four

WHAT ARE THEIR MOST USEFUL FEATURES?

Each air fryer has its own features from their cooking capacity to their settings. Be sure to consider these features when choosing your own air fryer, especially as your actual use of said features will contribute to its value for the money. Bells and whistles are good but when these add to the price and these will rarely, if ever, be used, then the air fryer isn't worth the money.

With that being said, here are three of the most useful and important features that you should look for in an air fryer.

COOKING CAPACITY

Look at the basket size first since it will affect the amount of food that the air fryer can be used with. The more people you're cooking for, the bigger the basket size should be obviously.

Keep this simple reference in mind when considering cooking capacity:

- 0.5-pound capacity – For a single person
- 1-pound capacity – For two persons
- 2- to 3-pound capacity – For a family, usually three to six persons

Since these are general estimates, you have to consider other factors, too. These include the types of food, the number of persons, and the amount of servings, among others. You may, for example, buy a family-sized air fryer in a two-person household when you usually have family and friends over during weekends.

Furthermore, the size and weight of an air fryer will be influenced by its cooking capacity. Size, which can refer to the depth of the cooking chamber, can vary from five inches to 40 inches with many commercial-sized air fryers being deeper than 40 inches.

Weight also varies from a lightweight 10 pounds to a heavyweight 20-plus pounds; a lighter air fryer is obviously best when you're planning on using it outside of the kitchen or when it will be stored in a tall cabinet. Also, check that the air fryer will fit into the countertop where you intend to use it.

TEMPERATURE RANGE

Cooking food with a too low or too high temperature can be disastrous, if not a waste of your money. Fortunately, most air fryers have adjustable temperatures ranging from 100°F to 400°F, as well as preset temperatures for certain foods and a temperature guide. Before using your new air fryer, read the instructions manual first since there will be valuable information in it, temperature- and time-wise.

In general, the higher the temperature range, the more foods that you can cook in an air fryer. But even with a lower temperature, food can still be cooked well albeit for a longer period.

Check the air fryer's temperature guide or the recipe for the proper temperature for whatever food you're cooking in it. Chicken nuggets and French fries, for example, will come out crispy at around 350°F. Pork chops and chicken breasts require higher temperatures, such as 400°F, and cook for longer periods for best results.

TIME SETTING

Cooking food for too long or too short periods can also be disastrous, palatability-wise. Just as with choosing the right temperature, it's important to set the right cook time on an air fryer.

Again, air fryers have adjustable time settings, usually ranging from 15 minutes to 60 minutes. The higher time settings can make up, so to speak, for the lower temperature options. As we previously mentioned, you can cook food at a lower temperature for a longer period and get similar results as when you cook it at a higher temperature for a shorter period.

Most digital air fryers also have pre-programmed settings for time and temperature. These are useful for people who value ease of use and convenience although these are usually only available in digital air fryers with touchscreen control panels. The settings typically includes pre-set time and temperature settings for common foods, such as French fries and onion rings, steaks and patties, and fried chicken.

But these are designed as general estimates so you have to determine the right settings, too. For example, you should obviously set a longer cook time when you're cooking a higher volume of food in an air fryer.

Air fryers also have several features that extend their usefulness in a modern kitchen. These features should also be considered when choosing an air fryer for your kitchen.

BUZZING TIMER

You will be alerted when the cook time is up with a buzzing sound. You should ideally remove the food from the air fryer lest it becomes overdone, perhaps even burned to a crisp.

TEMPERATURE LIGHT

You can see whether the air fryer has reached its desired temperature via the temperature light.

REMOVABLE BASKET AND PAN

You will have an easy time cleaning the basket and pan in the dishwasher, a must to avoid food and oil buildup in the cooking chamber.

COOKING TRAY AND/OR GRILL PAN INSERT

You can buy either or both of these removable accessories as part of a complete air fryer system or you may buy them separately. These can be considered as must-have accessories in case you're planning on expanding an air fryer's uses, such as from frying to grilling, roasting, and baking.

A cooking tray has a similar function as a toaster or oven tray. A grill pan insert is necessary for cooking meats and burgers.

No matter the features in your chosen air fryer, you have to try using all of them since you paid for them. Check out our recipes since these maximize the full range of your air fryer's features!

Chapter Five
WHAT ARE THE BENEFITS OF USING THEM?

Air fryers are popular kitchen appliances because of their safety, ease and convenience in use, and health benefits. But we must emphasize that the taste and texture between deep fried foods and air fried foods aren't the same, a fact that chefs like Gordon Ramsay agree with. This is because of the less oil used in air frying so the familiar deep fried taste won't be present.

There's good news, nonetheless: Even with just a tablespoon of oil, chips will be crispy on the outside and tender on the inside, as well as taste great. The chips are healthier, too, because of the less amount of oil used – and the health benefits are the main reason for their increasing popularity.

In the following section, we will take a closer look at the actual benefits of using air fryers on a regular basis.

REDUCED FAT CONTENT IN FOOD

Deep fried foods generally have higher fat content than foods cooked using other methods, such as grilling, broiling and steaming. As an example, a fried chicken breast will contain approximately 30% more fat than a roasted chicken breast. We even found some manufacturers of air fryers that claim using their products can cut fat content by up to 75% on fried foods!

We strongly agree because a typical air fryer will require about 1 teaspoon (15 ml) of oil for frying food like chicken, steak, and fish. In stark contrast, traditional deep fryers will require at least 3 cups (750 ml) of oil – and the difference in volume can mean the difference between a healthy heart and a plaque-riddled heart in the long run.

Of course, not all the oil in traditional deep frying will be absorbed by the food but the fact that there's a higher amount of oil used means that the fried foods will have higher fat content. Even when all the oil in an air fryer will be used up, the final fried food will still have lower fat content – truly, good news for health-conscious individuals.

Again, we have to emphasize that while there will be subtle flavor differences between deep-fried and air-fried foods, both will have a similar color, crispness and moisture content. French fries and potato chips will have a crunchy exterior and a flavorful interior while breaded pork chops will have crispy skin and juicy texture, for example.

With reduced fat content, many fans of air fryers say that the kitchen appliance was instrumental in their weight loss success. Air-fried foods, after all, also have reduced calorie content.

We must emphasize, nonetheless, that it's important to adopt other sensible food-related practices, too, such as portion control, healthy food choices, and more frequent yet smaller meals. Air-fried foods are only a part of a wholistic approach to weight loss, not the be-all and end-all of it.

DECREASED FORMATION OF POTENTIALLY HARMFUL COMPOUNDS

In traditional deep frying, the oil has to be heated well in order to make it suitable for frying and to get the desired Maillard effect. But studies have shown that heating oil can cause the formation of potentially harmful compounds including acrylamide, aldehydes, and polycyclic aromatic hydrocarbons, to name a few.

The International Agency for Research on Cancer classifies acrylamide as a "probable carcinogen", a term used to designate compounds with possible links to cancer. Acrylamide forms when carbohydrate-rich foods, such as sweet potatoes and potatoes, are cooked in high heat, as is the case in deep-frying.

Researchers from the University of the Basque Country in Spain have also discovered certain toxic aldehydes in fried foods. At temperature suitable for frying, oil will release aldehydes due to the degradation of the oil's fatty acids. Aldehydes are highly reactive compounds that react with hormones, enzymes and proteins in a living organism – the human body, in this case – contributing to its abnormal functioning.

This was true regardless of the type of vegetable oil used. In the same research, sunflower oil had the highest level of aldehydes compared with those found in olive oil and flaxseed oil.

Since only 1 tablespoon of oil is required for air-frying purposes, there's less risk of these potentially harmful compounds being absorbed by the air-fried foods. The result: You will be less likely to consume them, too, so your risks for cancer and other chromic degenerative diseases may also decrease.

Aside from these health benefits, we have also found other benefits from regular and proper use of air fryers.

FASTER COOKING TIMES

In most cases, air-frying foods can be faster than traditional deep-frying methods. Be sure to use the recommended cooking times, especially if you're a newbie to an air fryer, for best results. Many air fryers also come with cooking charts, sometimes even with guides in converting any recipe into an air fryer-suitable recipe.

SUITABLE FOR COMPACT SPACES

Unfortunately, not everybody can have commercial-sized, full-featured luxury kitchens. Compact, multipurpose and energy-efficient kitchen appliances are always welcome among people who live in more modest accommodations – and that's exactly what air fryers are!

We have seen air fryers in college dormitories, condominium units, and apartments where the kitchens are the size of a handkerchief, so to speak. We have seen them prominently displayed on compact countertops because of their frequent use, in contrast with other kitchen appliances gathering dust in overhead cabinets.

We have also seen them in luxury kitchens not because the owners or chefs are being stingy with space. Instead, these kitchen appliances are becoming increasingly popular among the rich and famous because of their numerous benefits.

MULTIPURPOSE FUNCTIONS

We have emphasized it several times because it's so true! Many types of air fryers can be used for other cooking methods aside from the usual frying.

Air fryers can be used for baking, roasting, grilling, pan frying, and sautéing, and re-heating. We have to say that it's easier to list what it cannot do – because there are so little of them - instead of what it can do! We have yet to use even top-of-the-line air fryer for making stews, soups, and cold salads although it can be used to make a few of the ingredients in a cold salad (e.g. roasted beets or potatoes).

EASE OF OPERATION

Air fryers are so easy to use that even a newbie cook can use them with flair! Many chefs who aren't into new kitchen gadgets also find them simple and convenient to use.

But don't be too complacent about using a brand-new air fryer even when you have used one before. Always read the instructions manual before operating it for the first time.

Air fryers are also safer than the standard pots and pans since there are no issues with grease and oil splatters. These are also more suitable for households where hot plates and/or stovetops pose high safety risks, such as when children are around.

EASE OF MAINTENANCE

With air fryers, there are no burnt bottoms and stubborn grease, which can be frustrating to remove with a scrub and mild detergent. Just wipe off the exterior parts with a dry, clean cloth and place the cooking chamber into the dishwasher, if applicable. There's no leftover oil to dispose, too.

With these benefits, air fryers are becoming the must-have kitchen appliances in restaurants and homes worldwide!

Chapter Six

WHAT ARE THE MOST IMPORTANT THINGS TO REMEMBER ABOUT THEIR USE?

Air fryers may be easy to use but there are still important things to keep in mind about these handy kitchen appliances! Since these are electronic appliances, safety is still a primary concern so we suggest reading the instructions manual about safety precautions. These can range from plugging in an air fryer into the right outlet to cooking the right types and amount of food.

The following tips are general in nature so these can be applied to all models of air fryers, such as the Phillips air fryer models. For more detailed instructions, we again suggest looking to the air fryer's user's manual.

FOODS SUITABLE FOR COOKING IN AIR FRYERS

Nearly all types of vegetables including green leafy vegetables and root crops; meats like chicken, pork, beef and turkey; fish and shellfish; and baked goods, among others, can be cooked in a standard air fryer. Even frozen foods can be cooked in it although certain steps should first be taken to prepare them. Foods that require a light flour coating or a bread crumb coating can also be fried in it,

There are foods, however, that shouldn't be cooked in air fryers because of the mediocre results, if not for safety reasons. These include veggies that can be steamed like beans and carrots. Better yet, check the instructions manual as many manufacturers include a list of dos and don'ts in food.

Regardless of the food being cooked inside an air fryer's cooking chamber, it should be kept as dry as possible. We suggest patting foods dry with a kitchen towel before placing them in the cooking chamber, such as with marinated foods. This will reduce the risk of splattering of liquids and excess smoke.

COOKING MULTIPLE DISHES SIMULTANEOUSLY

Multiple ingredients can be cooked simultaneously in a typical air fryer. But don't just place two types of food helter-skelter in its cooking chamber since it will affect the food's final results.

- Check the total capacity of the cooking chamber. Most air fryers have a 500-gram capacity so weigh the ingredients first, if necessary. Check the "Max" mark in the basket, too, and keep the food level within the line.
- Use the separator or divider in dividing the ingredients inside the pan or basket when cooking two foods at once. The divider is essential in proper cooking, aside from reducing the number of minutes it takes to cook the foods.

Be sure to check that, indeed, the two different ingredients require the same or similar cooking time and temperature, thus, they can cook evenly. A good example are potato wedges and chicken drumsticks.

In case two types of food don't have similar cooking requirements, it's still possible to cook them nearly at the same time in an air fryer. Place the food with the longer preparation time, close the cooking chamber, and let it cook for a while. Then, add the second food so that it can finish cooking at the same time as the first food.

Be quick when adding extra ingredients to the air fryer's cooking chamber. Otherwise, the heat loss from opening it may result in longer cooking times. Keep the second type of food on hand for this reason.

NOTES ON THE USE OF OIL

When there isn't sufficient oil in the air fryer for the type of food being cooked, the food will not have the Maillard effect – in other words, it will be less juicy and crispy than desired. In many of the recipes, we only recommend spraying on the oil of your choice on the air fryer's cooking chamber.

There's no best oil for use in an air fryer so you can use olive oil, grapeseed oil, avocado oil, peanut oil, and sunflower oil. We strongly suggest, nonetheless, using oils with a high smoke point because air fryers can have extremely high internal temperatures. With the air being blown about inside its cooking chamber, these also cannot ventilate smoke efficiently.

The smoke point, by the way, refers to the approximate temperature an oil starts to smoke. The higher the smoke point of a cooking oil, the more suitable it is for use in an air fryer. The best smoke point is 400°F and above so the following types of oil are recommended:

- Grapeseed oil (420°F)
- Palm oil (450°F)
- Peanut oil (450°F)
- Safflower oil (510°F)
- Rice bran oil (490°F)
- Soybean oil (450°F)
- Avocado oil (520°F)

Never use beef tallow, butter and ghee because these either have low smoke points or have solid states before being applied to the food.

A few tips to keep in mind when using any type of oil.

- Use oil sparingly. One to two tablespoons of oil are usually sufficient for foods with low natural oil content. The goals here are to prevent the food from sticking to the basket and to get the Maillard effect.
- Spray the air fryer's rack or basket lightly first when food that has been dredged or battered in flour will be cooked. Place the food in a single layer on the rack or basket then lightly spray with oil again; the second spray will make the food's surface turn golden brown and crispy.
- Brush oil on fish, meats and roasted vegetables instead of just spraying it on. In most stir-fried vegetable recipes, tossing the vegetables in a little oil is recommended.
- Spritz a light spray on the air fryer's rack before placing frozen and par-cooked foods, such as chicken strips and fish sticks, on it. Be sure to lightly spray the food, too. While these types of food can be cooked without added oil, a little oil will definitely be helpful.

We also suggest avoiding the preparation of fatty foods in the air fryer because of the risk of white smoke coming out of it. But if you must prepare them, we suggest using them as one of many ingredients, not as a single ingredient. For example, sausages can be used in a recipe but don't fry them as is in an air fryer.

USING PAPER AND FOIL

While either paper or foil can be used in an air fryer's cooking chamber, certain precautions must be kept in mind.

- Never completely cover the bottom of the basket with paper or foil. For proper cooking, there should be proper airflow for the steam to pass through easily. Otherwise, the reduced airflow decreases the air fryer's cooking performance.
- Never place paper or foil in the air fryer without placing food on top of it. Otherwise, the paper or foil will burn and stick to the bottom.
- Check that the paper or foil doesn't stick out beyond the edge of the basket.

Each air fryer model has specific instructions for using paper or foil but these recommendations apply to most models. Be sure to use only the pans, baskets and racks made specifically for the air fryer model, too, since these are designed for efficient air circulation.

SETTING THE COOKING TEMPERATURE

Pre-heating the air fryer isn't a requirement for proper cooking, unless otherwise noted in the recipe instructions. But pre-heating it for about four minutes can decrease cooking time –without the food yet, obviously. After pre-heating, be sure to set the temperature according to the recommended one in the recipe.

A note on converting the suggested temperature from cooking in conventional ovens to an air fryer: Reduce the air fryer's temperature by 25°F in relation to the conventional oven's temperature. This is also true when roasting food in an air fryer.

The adjustment is crucial in getting similar results. This is because the circulating air inside an air fryer makes for a more consistent cooking environment and, thus, it's more intense. The food will cook at lower temperatures due to the higher intensity of the cooking environment.

This tip is important because you will come across recipes that can be cooked in an air fryer but there are no instructions about cooking temperatures.

FILLING THE RACK OR BASKET WITH FOOD

Never overcrowd the air fryer's cooking chamber. The food should have plenty of space inside the cooking chamber so that air can effectively circulate and, thus, it can be cooked properly. Otherwise, the desired crispy results will not be achieved. The smaller the batch, the better it can be cooked.

Foods that have been battered and floured should ideally be arranged in a single layer only on the basket or rack. But in air fryers with racks that allow for two layers, the food can be placed in two layers.

Vegetables roasted in an air fryer and French fries can be loaded up to the top, if necessary. But keep in mind that a fuller basket will translate to longer cooking time and less crispy results. If you aren't pressed for time or you're cooking for a few people only, cooking in smaller batches is recommended.

When the food is already cooking, it's also necessary to open the air fryer and shake its contents for a few times. Shaking the food halfway through its cooking time ensures even cooking results, as well as allows for checking its color, crispiness and doneness. This is especially true for ingredients that touch each other – without shaking, some parts won't have the desired crispy results.

We recommend shaking the food every 5-10 minutes depending on its type. The process itself can either be manual or automatic depending on the air fryer's design.

In manual shaking, pull the pan out of the air fryer using its handle and then shake it gently. Check that the food has been mixed well before placing the pan back into the air fryer. In the case of French fries, for example, the lower layer should be on top after shaking so that it will be crispy.

In automatic shaking, you can let the air fryer do the work. The rotation of the food will be accomplished by its built-in food agitator that churns the ingredients on a continuous or regular basis.

In the following section, we take a look at air fryer-suitable recipes good for your 30-day meal planning. We chose these recipes because these are easy to prepare yet deliver on delicious and nutritious – in other words, short and sweet – that even the busiest housewife or househusband, career professional, and college student can whip up!

Part Two

BREAKFAST RECIPES

CHEESY AND PEPPERY VEGETABLE OMELET

Preparation Time: 15 Minutes | Servings: 2

Nutrition Info (per serving)
Calories: 380 | Fat: 30 g | Protein: 16 g | Carbs: 5 g

INGREDIENTS:

- 4 eggs; whisked
- 3 tablespoons plain milk
- 1 teaspoon melted butter
- Salt and black pepper according to your taste
- 1 red bell pepper; remove seeds, stem and vein before chopping
- 1 green bell pepper; remove seeds, stem and vein before chopping
- 1 white onion; chopped finely
- ½ cup baby spinach leaves; chopped roughly
- ½ cup shaved Halloumi cheese (or any cheese of your choice)

INSTRUCTIONS:

1. Spray oil into the air fryer baking pan.
2. Add all the ingredients into the pan and stir them well.
3. Close the pan and set the temperature for 350°F.
4. Cook for 13 minutes.
5. Serve warm.

TOMATO AND SPINACH SCRAMBLED EGGS

Preparation Time: 20 minutes | Servings: 2

Nutrition Info (per serving)
Calories: 262 | Fat: 16 g | Protein: 30 g | Carbs: 17 g

INGREDIENTS:

- 2 tablespoons olive oil
- 4 eggs; whisked
- 1 medium-sized tomato; chopped
- 8 ½ ounces fresh spinach; chopped
- 1 teaspoon fresh lemon juice
- Coarse salt and ground black pepper to taste
- ½ cup of fresh basil; chopped roughly

INSTRUCTIONS:

1. Preheat the air fryer for 4 minutes.
2. Evenly spray olive oil into the entire surface of the pan.
3. Combine all the ingredients except for the olive oil and basil leaves. Whisk well so there are no egg whites visible and the ingredients are well-incorporated.
4. Pour into the pan and cook for 8-12 minutes at 280°F.
5. Place the scrambled eggs into a plate, garnish with the chopped basil leaves, and serve; a dollop of sour cream can be served on the side, too, if desired.

EASY EGG BREAKFAST

Preparation Time: 25 minutes | Servings: 2

Nutrition Info (per serving)
Calories: 178 | Fat: 13 g | Protein: 32 g | Carbs: 12 g

INGREDIENTS:

- 2 tablespoons oil
- 2 eggs
- 2 cups all-purpose flour; sift, if desired
- 2 teaspoons baking powder
- 1 teaspoon baking soda
- 1 tablespoon brown sugar
- 1 teaspoon cinnamon powder
- 1 cup pumpkin puree
- 2 tablespoons vinegar
- ½ cup milk

INSTRUCTIONS:

1. Preheat air fryer to 300°F for 5 minutes.
2. Whisk the eggs in a bowl.
3. In another bowl, combine the dry ingredients – flour, baking soda, brown sugar, baking powder, and cinnamon powder. Stir a few times to combine well.
4. Make a well in the middle of the dry ingredients and add the wet

ingredients – whisked eggs, pumpkin puree, milk, and vinegar. Mix both types of ingredients until smooth but don't over-mix it; a few lumps is okay.
5. Grease the baking tray with the oil and pour the mixture.
6. Cook it for 10 minutes or until done.
7. Serve warm.

TOASTIES AND SAUSAGE SURPRISE

Preparation Time: 30 minutes | Servings: 2

Nutrition Info (per serving)
Calories: 130 | Fat: 4 g | Protein: 6 g | Carbs: 20 g

INGREDIENTS:

- ¼ cup milk or cream
- 2 sausages; sliced
- 3 eggs
- 1 piece bread; sliced lengthwise
- 4 tablespoons grated cheddar cheese (or any cheese of your choice)
- Salt and pepper to taste

INSTRUCTIONS:

1. Preheat the air fryer for 5 minutes at 360°F.
2. In a bowl, whisk the eggs and add the milk or cream until mixed well.
3. Grease 3 muffin cups with cooking spray. Check that the muffin cups fit into the air fryer.
4. Pour equal amounts of the egg-and-milk mixture into the muffin cups.
5. Arrange the bread and sausage slices – equal amounts, too – in the mixture. Use your fingers to press them deeply into the muffin cups.
6. Sprinkle with the grated cheese.

7. Place the muffin cups into the air fryer's cooking chamber.
8. Set the temperature to 360°F and let the mixture cook for 15-20 minutes.
9. Remove the cooked mixture from the muffin cups, serve them on a plate, and garnish with your choice in fresh herbs and/or steamed vegetables like broccoli.

PARSLEY AND SPINACH BAKED OMELET

Preparation Time: 15 minutes | Servings: 1

Nutrition Info (per serving)
Calories: 153 | Fat: 10 g | Protein: 15 g | Carbs: 3 g

INGREDIENTS:

- 1 teaspoon olive oil
- 3 eggs
- 3 tablespoons ricotta cheese
- 1 tablespoon chopped parsley
- ¼ cup chopped baby spinach leaves
- Salt and pepper to taste

INSTRUCTIONS:

1. Preheat the air fryer to 330°F for 4 minutes.
2. Spray the oil into the baking pan afterwards.
3. Whisk the eggs; be sure to season with salt and pepper.
4. Combine the parsley, spinach and ricotta cheese with the whisked eggs.
5. Pour the egg mixture on the greased pan and cook for 10 minutes.
6. Enjoy with your favorite bacon or sausage.

EASY-PEASY CHEESY OMELET

Preparation Time: 30 minutes | Servings: 2

Nutrition Info (per serving)
Calories: 244 | Fat: 23 g | Protein: 14 g | Carbs: 2 g

INGREDIENTS:

- Cooking spray
- 1 large onion; chopped finely
- 2 tablespoons grated cheddar cheese
- 3 large eggs
- ½ teaspoon soy sauce
- Salt and pepper powder according to your taste

INSTRUCTIONS:

1. Whisk the eggs, soy sauce, and salt and pepper together until blended well.
2. Spray the air fryer's pan with cooking spray.
3. Place the chopped onions into the pan. Place the pan into the air fryer and cook the onion for 6 minutes at 355°F.
4. Open the pan and pour the egg mixture over the now-translucent onions.
5. Sprinkle the grated cheese over the mixture.
6. Cook for another 5 minutes.
7. Serve the cooked eggs with your choice in bread.

BRAZILIAN TURKEY PIES

Preparation Time: 25 minutes | Serves: 4

Nutrition Info (per serving)
Calories: 221 | Fat: 3 g | Protein: 26 g | Carbs: 20 g

INGREDIENTS:

- 8 sheets filo pastry
- 1 ¾ ounce shredded turkey
- 1 egg; whisked
- 3 ½ tablespoon coconut milk
- 3 ½ tablespoon whole milk
- 5/6 cup tomato sauce
- 1 ½ tablespoon turkey stock
- 1 teaspoon oregano
- 1 tablespoon coriander
- Salt and pepper to taste
- Flour for lining the muffin cases

INSTRUCTIONS:

1. In a large bowl, mix all the wet ingredients except for the eggs – coconut milk, whole milk, tomato sauce, and turkey stock – and mix well.
2. Combine the shredded turkey, oregano, coriander, and salt and pepper to the liquid mixture. Set aside.

3. Line the muffin pie cases with a little flour to prevent the pies from sticking to the sides. In each case, place two sheets of filo pastry so that the sides are completely covered; the filo pastry hanging over the sides will be used to cover the top of the pie just before baking.
4. Pour the mixture into each case until it is ¾ full. Cover the top with the excess pastry hanging over the side.
5. Place the cases into the air fryer and cook the mixture for 10 minutes at 360°F.
6. Let the cooked pies cool down for 10 minutes before removing them from their cases and serving them on a plate.

EASY-PEASY ENGLISH-STYLE BREAKFAST

Preparation Time: 35 minutes | Servings: 2

Nutrition Info (per serving)
Calories: 419 | Fat: 24 g | Protein: 19 g | Carbs: 47 g

INGREDIENTS:

- 1 tablespoon olive oil
- 2 medium-sized potatoes, peeled and diced (or a cup of diced potatoes)
- 2 cups canned beans of your choice in light tomato sauce
- 2 eggs
- 1 sausage, sliced into bite-sized pieces
- Salt and pepper to taste

INSTRUCTIONS:

1. Preheat the air fryer to 390°F.
2. In an oven-safe dish, crack the eggs and add a pinch of salt and pepper.
3. In a medium-sized bowl, combine the diced potatoes and olive oil well; add a pinch of salt, too.
4. Place the coated potatoes into the air fryer and cook for 10 minutes.
5. Cover the half-cooked potatoes with parchment paper and add the eggs and beans on top; the paper will separate the two types of food.

6. Cook the three food for another 10 minutes.
7. Place the sliced sausage with the eggs and beans. Cook for 5 minutes more.
8. Serve the cooked food with toast and coffee.

SLOPPY JOE STUFFED SCONES

Preparation Time: 30 minutes | Servings: 4

Nutrition Info (per serving)
Calories: 304 | Fat: 19 g | Protein: 24 g | Carbs: 9 g

INGREDIENTS:

- 1 ¾ ounce Sloppy Joes
- 5/6 ounce butter
- 7/8 cup self-rising flour
- 5/6 ounce cheddar cheese, grated
- 1 cup plain milk
- 4 slices of cheese
- 1 egg
- 5 tablespoon oregano
- Salt and pepper to taste

INSTRUCTIONS:

1. Preheat the air fryer to 320°F.
2. To make the scones, combine the butter and self-rising flour in a medium-sized bowl until the dough mixture resembles breadcrumbs.
3. Add the egg, milk, and grated cheese into the dough mixture. Add more milk in case the dough still feels hard and dry; gradually

incorporate the milk, too, since it's easier to add a little more milk than to keep adding flour.
4. Separate the dough mixture into four and shape each one into a scone.
5. Place the four scones into the air fryer and bake for 15 minutes at 320°F.
6. Remove the scones from the air fryer and let them cool down.
7. Using a knife, slice off the top of each scone and then create a space in the center.
8. Mix the scone crumbs from the center with the Sloppy Joes mix.
9. Spoon the mixture into the crater of the scones.
10. Place the sliced-off top back into the scone and decorate it with a slice of cheese.
11. Bake in the air fryer for another 5 minutes and then serve.

APRICOT AND FRENCH TOAST DELIGHT

Preparation Time: 10 minutes | Servings: 6

Nutrition Info (per serving)
Calories: 198 | Fat: 5 g | Protein: 14 g | Carbs: 30 g

INGREDIENTS:

- 6 slices of French bread
- 2 tablespoons butter; soft but not melted
- 3 eggs
- 1/3 cup plain milk
- ¼ cup dried apricots, chopped finely
- A pinch of ground all-spice
- Powdered sugar for garnish

INSTRUCTIONS:

1. Preheat the air fryer to 380°F.
2. Spread butter on both sides of each slice of the French bread; set aside on a plate first.
3. Whisk the eggs, milk, egg spice and salt to taste in a medium-sized bowl.
4. Soak the buttered slices of French bread in the milk mixture for 10 minutes; don't over-soak.
5. Transfer the bread slices into the preheated air fryer baking dish.
6. Place the chopped apricots on top of the bread slices.

7. Spray a small amount of oil on top.
8. Cook the slices for 2 minutes.
9. Flip the bread slices, spray the top with oil, and the cook for another 3 minutes.
10. Place the bread slices into a plate, dust with powdered sugar, and serve with your choice in morning beverage.

ZUCCHINI AND CARROT MUFFINS

Preparation Time: 25 minutes | Servings: 4

Nutrition Info (per serving)
Calories: 91 | Fat: 5 g | Protein: 3 g | Carbs: 32 g

INGREDIENTS:

- 1 ½ cups all-purpose flour, sifted
- 2 tablespoons sugar
- 2 teaspoon baking powder
- 1 cup plain milk
- 2 tablespoons melted butter
- 2 tablespoons cream cheese
- 3 eggs
- 1 tablespoon yogurt
- A pinch of salt
- ½ cup shredded zucchini
- ¼ cup shredded carrots

INSTRUCTIONS:

1. Preheat the air fryer to 350°F.
2. Combine the dry ingredients – flour, sugar, baking powder, and salt – first in a medium-sized bowl.
3. Combine the wet ingredients – milk, melted butter, cream cheese, eggs, and yogurt – in another bowl.

4. Whisk the dry mixture into the wet mixture gradually until well-incorporated; don't over-mix since small lumps are acceptable.
5. Fold the shredded carrots and zucchini into the batter.
6. Grease the muffins tins.
7. Pour the batter into the tins until ¾ full.
8. Bake in the air fryer for 12-14 minutes until done.
9. Serve with whipped cream, if desired.

PECAN AND PUMPKIN MUFFINS

Preparation Time: 25 minutes | Servings: 4

Nutrition Info (per serving)
Calories:336 | Fat: 13 g | Protein: 5 g | Carbs: 57 g

INGREDIENTS:

- 4 tablespoons cake flour
- ¼ cup oats
- 1/3 teaspoon baking powder
- A pinch of salt

- ¼ cup ghee
- ¼ cup caster sugar
- ¼ cup pumpkin puree
- 2 tablespoons ground pecans

- ½ teaspoon freshly grated nutmeg
- ¼ teaspoon ground cinnamon
- ¼ teaspoon crystalized ginger

INSTRUCTIONS:

1. Preheat the air fryer to 320°F.
2. Mix the cake flour, oats, and baking powder with a pinch of salt (i.e., dry mixture) in a medium-sized bowl.

3. In another bowl, whisk the ghee with the sugar, then gradually fold in the pumpkin puree and ground pecans into it, and stir a few times (i.e., wet mixture).
4. Add the dry mixture to the wet mixture and mix well.
5. Mix the nutmeg, cinnamon, and ginger to the final mix; use a wide spatula to mix these spices.
6. Place muffin molds to the muffin tins.
7. Pour the mixture into the muffin tins until they are ¾ full.
8. Bake in the air fryer for 10 minutes at 320°F.
9. Let the muffins cool after baking before removing them from their molds.

SAVORY CORN AND SCALLION CAKES

Preparation Time: 20 minutes | Servings: 6

Nutrition Info (per serving)
Calories: 235 | Fat: 7 g | Protein: 11 g | Carbs: 32 g

INGREDIENTS:

- 1 ¼ cups all-purpose flour
- 1 teaspoon baking powder
- ½ teaspoon baking soda
- 1 teaspoon paprika
- ¼ teaspoon sugar
- Pinch of salt
- Pinch of freshly-grated nutmeg

- ¼ teaspoon white vinegar
- 1 ½ tablespoons melted butter
- ½ cup milk
- 1 egg

- 1 ¼ cups corn kernels
- ¼ cup chopped cilantro
- ¼ cup chopped scallions

INSTRUCTIONS:

1. Preheat the air fryer to 380°F.
2. In a medium-sized bowl, combine the dry ingredients – flour, baking powder, baking soda, paprika, sugar, salt, and nutmeg.
3. In another mixing bowl, mix the wet ingredients – vinegar, melted butter, egg, and milk.
4. Add the wet mixture to the dry mixture; stir a few times to incorporate the two mixtures well.
5. Stir in the cilantro, scallions, and corn kernels into the combined mixture.
6. Make rounded fritters from the batter and then chill them in the freezer for 5 minutes.
7. Place them into the air fryer and cook for 5 minutes at 380°F.
8. Remove from the air fryer and serve warm with your choice of dip, such as mayonnaise.

FAST BREAKFAST SHRIMP TOASTS

Preparation Time: 30 minutes | Servings: 4

Nutrition Info (per serving)
Calories: 90 | Fat: 3 g | Protein: 5 g | Carbs: 6 g

INGREDIENTS:

- ¾ pound large raw shrimps, peeled, deveined and chopped
- 1 egg white
- 2 tablespoons cornstarch
- 3 cloves of garlic
- Salt and pepper to taste
- 4 Slices of white bread
- Olive oil

INSTRUCTIONS:

1. Preheat the air fryer to 370°F.
2. Combine the shrimp, egg white, cornstarch, garlic, and salt and pepper in a mixing bowl.
3. Spread the shrimp mixture in a thin layer over the bread slices.
4. Sprinkle the top with olive oil.
5. Place the bread slices in the air fryer's basket.
6. Cook them for 10 minutes until lightly brown and crispy.

CARROT, CUCUMBER AND SALMON MIX

Preparation Time: 25 minutes | Servings: 2

Nutrition Info (per serving)
Calories: 78 | Fat: 3 g | Protein: 7 g | Carbs: 18 g

INGREDIENTS:

- 1 pound salmon, chopped into bite-sized pieces
- 4 white bread slices
- 1 medium-sized carrot, shredded
- 2 medium-sized cucumbers, sliced
- 2 cups feta cheese, crumbled
- 3 tablespoons pickled red onion

INSTRUCTIONS:

1. Combine the chopped salmon and crumbled feta in a mixing bowl.
2. Add the pickled red onion, carrot, and cucumbers and mix well.
3. Layer the 4 bread slices into the air fryer's cooking chamber; be sure to cover all the surface.
4. Pour the salmon and vegetables mixture over the bread slices; arrange for an even layer.
5. Cook in the air fryer for 15 minutes at 300°F.

BASIC BREAKFAST DONUTS

Preparation Time: 1 hour and 20 minutes | Servings: 6

Nutrition Info (per serving)
Calories: 289 | Fat: 9 g | Protein: 16 g | Carbs: 40 g

INGREDIENTS:

- 1 cup white all-purpose flour, sifted
- 1 teaspoon baking powder
- ¼ cup coconut sugar
- ½ teaspoon salt
- ¼ teaspoon cinnamon
- 1 tablespoon coconut oil; melted
- ¼ cup almond milk
- 2 tablespoon aquafaba or liquid from canned chickpeas

INSTRUCTIONS:

1. Mix well the flour, baking powder, and coconut sugar as well as the salt and cinnamon (i.e., dry ingredients) in a mixing bowl.
2. Mix well the coconut oil, almond milk, and aquafaba in another bowl.
3. Gradually mix the dry ingredients into the wet ingredients. Use a spatula to combine the ingredients well until a sticky dough is created.
4. Place the dough in the refrigerator for an hour to rest.

5. Create small balls from the dough – use an ice cream scooper for equal dough amounts - and set aside.
6. Preheat the air fryer to 370°F.
7. Place the dough balls into the air fryer and cook for 10 minutes.
8. Once cooked, take the basic donuts out of the air fryer.
9. Sprinkle with cinnamon and sugar, or any other sweet or savory topping desired.

Cooking tip: Don't shake the donuts when these are cooking in the air fryer; just let them be for 10 minutes. This will maintain the shape of the donuts.

SPICY CHICKEN, VEGETABLES, AND SHELL SPAGHETTI SPECIAL

Preparation Time: 25 minutes | Servings: 3

Nutrition Info (per serving)
Calories: 308 | Fat: 11 g | Protein: 19 g | Carbs: 38 g

INGREDIENTS:

- 1 tablespoon canola oil
- 2 pieces boneless and skinless chicken breast, chopped into bite-sized pieces
- 2 cloves garlic, minced
- 2 tablespoons chili paste
- ½ cup soy sauce
- 2 small carrots, cut into cubes
- 1 medium-sized onion, sliced
- 1 small head broccoli, cut into smaller florets
- ½ cabbage, julienned
- Salt and pepper to taste
- Ginger, grated, to taste
- 2 pounds shell spaghetti
- Grated cheese, to taste

INSTRUCTIONS:

1. Grease the baking tray with the canola oil.
2. In a mixing bowl, combine the chicken, garlic, chili paste, soy sauce,

carrots, onion, cabbage, and ginger. Stir a few times for an even distribution of the ingredients.
3. Pour the mixed ingredients into the air fryer's tray and cook for 15 minutes at 300°F.
4. Cook the shell spaghetti according to package instructions while waiting for the topping to cook.
5. Combine the shell spaghetti and the topping on a large plate, top with your choice in cheese, and serve.

VEGAN TACO CRISP WRAPS

Preparation Time: 30 minutes | Servings: 4

Nutrition Info (per serving)
Calories: 175 | Fat: 7 g | Protein: 11 g | Carbs: 22 g

INGREDIENTS:

- 1 tablespoon water
- 4 pieces vegan nuggets, chopped; Buy these from a supermarket
- 1 yellow onion, diced
- 1 red bell pepper; chopped
- 2 cobs grilled corn kernels
- 4 large tortillas

INSTRUCTIONS:

1. Preheat the air fryer to 400°F.
2. Heat a skillet over medium heat.
3. Saute the vegan nuggets, onions, bell pepper and corn kernels in water for a few minutes. Let the filling cool for a few minutes.
4. Place an equal amount of the filling in each of the large tortilla.
5. Fold the tortilla so that it looks like a spring roll; do the same for all 4 tortillas.
6. Place in the air fryer and cook for 15 minutes. The tortilla should be crispy afterwards.
7. Serve the crisp wraps with mix greens or meat-based dip.

EASY VEGETABLE PASTA SALAD WITH BALSAMIC VINEGAR DRESSING

Preparation Time: 30 minutes | Servings: 6

Nutrition Info (per serving)
Calories: 35 | Fat: 1 g | Protein: 1 g | Carbs: 5 g

INGREDIENTS:

- 1 medium-sized zucchini, sliced into thin semicircles
- 1 small butternut squash, sliced into semicircles
- 1 red onion, sliced into semicircles
- 3 bell peppers – red, green, and orange – chopped roughly
- 1 cup mushrooms, sliced roughly
- 1 teaspoon Italian seasoning
- 4 teaspoons olive oil
- Salt and pepper to taste

- 1 pound of penne rigate or rigatoni pasta, cooked
- 1 cup cherry tomatoes, cut in half
- ½ cup olives, pitted and halved
- 3 tablespoons balsamic vinegar
- Fresh basil, minced, to taste

INSTRUCTIONS:

1. Preheat the air fryer for minutes to 380°F.

2. In a bowl, mix the zucchini, butternut squash, onion, bell peppers, mushroom, and Italian seasoning.
3. Pour 2 tablespoons of olive oil over the mixed vegetables and stir a few times to mix well.
4. Place the mixed vegetables into the air fryer basket and cook for 12-14 minutes depending on your desired level of doneness.
5. Shake the basket at the halfway mark.
6. Let the roasted mixed vegetables cool for a few minutes and transfer to a bowl.
7. Combine the mixed vegetables with the cooked pasta, olives, and cherry tomatoes as well as the balsamic vinegar and 2 tablespoons of olive oil.
8. Toss well while adding salt and black pepper to taste.
9. Sprinkle with fresh basil before serving.

ITALIAN CHICKEN-FLAVORED CHEESY RISOTTO

Preparation Time: 40 minutes | Servings: 2

Nutrition Info (per serving)
Calories: 210 | Fat: 6 g | Protein: 6 g | Carbs: 35 g

INGREDIENTS:

- 1 tablespoon unsalted butter
- 1 white onion, diced
- 1 clove garlic, minced
- ¾ cup Arborio rice
- 2 cups chicken stock
- ½ cup grated cheddar or parmesan cheese

INSTRUCTIONS:

1. Preheat the air fryer for 5 minutes at 390°F.
2. Grease an air fryer-suitable baking tin with olive oil.
3. Place the butter, onion and garlic into the greased baking tin and stir a few times.
4. Adjust the air fryer's timer to 8 minutes when it's already hot.
5. Place the baking tin into the air fryer and cook the food in it for 4 minutes.
6. Add the rice and cook for 4 minutes.
7. Open the air fryer's cooking chamber to stir the food; do so for 3 times during the cooking process.

8. Decrease the air fryer's temperature to 320°F and set its timer to 22 minutes.
9. Open the air fryer's cooking chamber and pour the chicken stock into the rice mixture. Stir gently.
10. Cook the rice mixture for 22 minutes but don't cover the air fryer.
11. Add the grated cheese, stir a few times, and serve.

KID-FRIENDLY SPINACH BALLS

Preparation Time: 25 minutes | Servings: 4

Nutrition Info (per serving)
Calories: 37 | Fat: 2 g | Protein: 2 g | Carbs: 3 g

INGREDIENTS:

- 1 medium-sized carrot; peeled and grated
- 1 package fresh baby spinach leaves; blanched and chopped
- ½ red onion; chopped finely
- 1 egg, whisked
- ½ teaspoon garlic powder
- 2 cloves garlic; minced
- 1 teaspoon salt
- ½ teaspoon black pepper
- 1 tablespoon yeast
- 1 tablespoon corn flour
- ½ cup bread crumbs

INSTRUCTIONS:

1. In a large bowl, evenly mix all the ingredients except for the crumbs.
2. Make small equally-sized balls from the mixture.
3. Roll the balls over the bread crumbs to achieve an even coating.
4. Spray oil into the air fryer's pan and place the spinach balls in it.
5. Cook the spinach balls at 390°F for 10 minutes.

POTATO BREAD ROLLS

Preparation Time: 30 minutes | Servings: 5

Nutrition Info (per serving)
Calories: 70 | Fat: 1 g | Protein: 5 g | Carbs: 17 g

INGREDIENTS:

- 5 large baking potatoes, peeled and boiled
- 1 tablespoon olive oil
- 2 small red onions, chopped finely
- ½ teaspoon mustard seeds
- ½ teaspoon turmeric powder
- 2 sprigs of curry leaves
- 1 bunch of coriander, chopped finely
- 2 green chilies, seeded and chopped
- 8 slices of wheat bread with the brown sides discarded

INSTRUCTIONS:

1. Preheat the air fryer at 400°F for f minutes.
2. In a bowl, mash the boiled potatoes and add salt and pepper according to your taste. Set aside.
3. In a skillet placed over medium heat, heat the olive oil and add the mustard seeds. Be sure to stir the mustard seeds so these don't burn.
4. When the mustard seeds start to sputter, add the onions and continue stirring.

5. When the onions are translucent, add the curry leaves and turmeric powder. Cook for 2 minutes more and remove the skillet from the stove.
6. Mix the potatoes, green chilies, and coriander to make the filling. Stir a few times to incorporate the spices into the mashed potatoes.
7. Sprinkle or spray the bread slices with water just enough to ensure a moist crumb.
8. Place a tablespoon of the potato mixture into the center of the bread. Roll the bread similar to rolling spring rolls; ensure that the bread completely covers the potato mixture.
9. Brush the bread with oil.
10. Place in the air fryer's basket and cook for 15 minutes at 400°F.

Cooking tip: Gently shake the air fryer basket halfway through the 15-minute time to ensure even cooking.

CHEESY POTATO WEDGES

Preparation Time: 15 minutes | Servings: 4

Nutrition Info (per serving)
Calories: 410 | Fat: 25 g | Protein: 8 g | Carbs: 40 g

INGREDIENTS:

- 1 pound fingerling potatoes, peeled and cut into large wedges
- 1 teaspoon extra virgin olive oil
- ½ teaspoon garlic powder
- Salt and pepper to taste
- Jarred cheese sauce

INSTRUCTIONS:

1. Preheat the air fryer to 400°F.
2. In a bowl, mix the potato wedges with the garlic powder, olive oil, and salt and pepper. Using your hands, toss the potatoes so these are coated with the olive oil.
3. Place the potatoes in the air fryer basket; arrange so that these can be evenly cooked.
4. Cook for 10 minutes at 400°F.
5. Serve with a generous ladling of cheese sauce, drizzled on top of the potato wedges and on the side for dipping.

HOMEMADE VEGETABLE PIZZA ON TOAST

Preparation Time: 30 minutes | Servings: 4

Nutrition Info (per serving)
Calories: 310 | Fat: 9 g | Protein: 13 g | Carbs: 44 g

INGREDIENTS:

- 4 slices Italian or Italian bread, buttered and toasted for 2-4 minutes
- 1 red bell pepper, julienned
- 1 cup sliced mushrooms; button or cremini mushrooms are preferred
- 1 small squash, sliced into thin strips or squares
- 2 green onions, sliced in semicircles
- 1 tablespoon olive oil
- 2 tablespoon butter, softened
- ½ cup goat cheese, softened

INSTRUCTIONS:

1. Spray the air fryer's basket with olive oil.
2. Preheat the air fryer to 350°F.
3. Place the bell pepper, mushrooms, green onions, and squash into the preheated basket. Mix them well and cook for 7 minutes at 350°F. Shake the basket once during the halfway mark.
4. Transfer the cooked vegetable topping to a plate and set aside.
5. Spread softened goat cheese on the toasted bread slices.
6. Top with the cooked vegetables and serve warm.

YUMMY MAPLE CINNAMON BUNS

Preparation Time: 2 hours | Servings: 9

Nutrition Info (per serving)
Calories: 260 | Fat: 3 g | Protein: 4 g | Carbs: 46 g

INGREDIENTS:

- ¾ cup tablespoon almond milk, unsweetened
- 4 tablespoons maple syrup
- 1 ½ tablespoon active yeast

- 3 tablespoons water
- 1 tablespoon ground flaxseed
- 1 tablespoon coconut oil, melted and cooled

- 1 ½ cup white flour, sifted
- 1 cup whole grain flour, sifted
- 2 tablespoons cinnamon powder

- ½ cup pecan nuts, toasted
- 2 ripe bananas, sliced in semicircles
- 4 dates, pitted
- ¼ cup icing sugar

INSTRUCTIONS:

1. Place the almond milk on a skillet and heat it until it's lukewarm only. Transfer to a small bowl.
2. Add the yeast and maple syrup to the almond milk; let the yeast mixture sit for 5-10 minutes to activate the yeast.
3. In another bowl, mix the water and ground flaxseed and then allow it (i.e., flaxseed mixture) to soak for 2 minutes.
4. Add the coconut oil to the flaxseed mixture.
5. Combine the yeast and flaxseed mixtures in one bowl.
6. In another bowl, mix the plain white flour and whole grain flour with 1 tablespoon cinnamon powder. Mix well for even distribution.
7. Pour the yeast-and-flaxseed mixture into the flour mixture to create the dough.
8. Scatter flour on a flat surface, such as a kitchen counter, and knead the dough on it. Knead it for 10 minutes.
9. Grease a bowl and place the kneaded dough in it. Cover the bowl with a kitchen towel and leave it in a warm, dark area for an hour.
10. Make the cinnamon bun filling by mixing the banana slices, pecans, and dates as well as 1 tablespoon cinnamon.
11. Preheat the air fryer to 390°F.
12. Scatter a handful of dough on a flat surface. Using a baking roller, roll the dough on it until it's thin.
13. Spread evenly the pecan filling on the dough's surface.
14. Using your hands, slowly roll the dough into itself to form a long roll with the pecan filling inside it.
15. Cut the rolled dough into nine slices.
16. Place inside the air fryer's basket and cook for 30 minutes at 390°F.
17. Sprinkle with icing sugar before serving.

CHEESY VEGETABLE BREAKFAST FRITTATA

Preparation Time: 35 minutes | Servings: 2

Nutrition Info (per serving)
Calories: 198 | Fat: 13 g | Protein: 13 g | Carbs: 6 g

INGREDIENTS:

- 4 large eggs
- ¼ cup plain milk
- 1 small zucchini, sliced
- ½ cup button mushrooms, sliced
- 1 large red onion, sliced
- ½ bunch asparagus
- ½ cup baby spinach
- ½ tablespoon olive oil
- 4 tablespoons grated cheddar cheese
- 5 tablespoons feta cheese, crumbled into small chunks
- ¼ bunch chives, minced
- Salt and pepper to taste

INSTRUCTIONS:

1. Whisk the eggs and milk in a hollow dish; season with salt and pepper to taste.
2. Heat a non-stick pan, place the olive oil in it, and sauté the zucchini, mushrooms, asparagus, spinach, and red onions. Stir frying the

vegetables should be for 5-7 minutes over medium heat only to preserve their texture and flavor.
3. Cover the air fryer's basket with parchment paper and place the sautéed vegetables and egg-milk mixture into it.
4. Sprinkle the combined ingredients with grated cheese and feta cheese.
5. Preheat the air fryer for 5 minutes at 320°F.
6. Place the baking tin with its ingredients in the air fryer.
7. Cook the frittata for 5 minutes at 390°F.
8. Garnish the cooked frittata with minced chives and serve.

QUICK CHEDDAR AND BACON QUICHE

Preparation Time: 30 minutes | Servings: 4

Nutrition Info (per serving)
Calories: 60 | Fat: 4 g | Protein: 3 g | Carbs: 9 g

INGREDIENTS:

- 1 short crust pastry, divided into 8 equal pieces
- 3 tablespoons Greek yogurt
- ¾ cup bacon, chopped
- ½ cup grated cheddar cheese
- 4 eggs, whisked
- ¼ teaspoon garlic powder
- ¼ teaspoon onion powder
- Salt and pepper to taste
- Flour for sprinkling

INSTRUCTIONS:

1. Preheat the air fryer to 330°F.
2. Grease 8 ramekins with oil and coat them with a thin layer of flour. Be sure to tap off the excess flour.
3. In each ramekin, place a piece of the short crust pastry so that most of its surface is covered.
4. In a bowl, mix the ingredients for the filling – yogurt, bacon, cheddar

cheese, eggs, garlic and onion powder, and salt and pepper. Stir to incorporate them well.
5. Pour equal amounts of the filling into the pastry-lined ramekins.
6. Place the ramekins into the air fryer and cook the quiche for 20 minutes at 330°F.

SUMPTUOUS BEGINNER'S SOUFFLÉ

Preparation Time: 25 minutes | Servings: 4

Nutrition Info (per serving)
Calories: 115 | Fat: 4 g | Protein: 10 g | Carbs: 15 g

INGREDIENTS:

- ¼ cup all-purpose flour, sifted
- 1/3 cup butter, softened but not melted
- 1 cup plain milk
- ¼ cup brown sugar
- 4 egg yolks
- 6 egg whites
- 1 teaspoon vanilla extract
- 2 tablespoons white sugar
- 1 teaspoon cream of tartar

INSTRUCTIONS:

1. Preheat the air fryer to 330°F.
2. In a bowl, combine the flour and butter until a smooth mixture is created. Set aside.
3. In a saucepan, heat the milk and add the brown sugar until it's dissolved. Bring the mixture to a boil on low heat.
4. Add the flour-butter mixture to the milk-sugar mixture. Be sure to beat the two mixtures vigorously to prevent lump formation.

5. Simmer the two mixtures for 7 minutes or until it thickens.
6. Remove from heat and let it cool for 15-20 minutes.
7. Coat 6 soufflé dishes with oil spray.
8. In a separate bowl, beat the egg yolks and vanilla extract for a minute or so,
9. Add in the cooled-down milk-and-flour mixture.
10. In a separate bowl, beat the white sugar, egg whites, and cream of tartar until well-incorporated.
11. Fold the egg white mixture into the base of the soufflé dishes.
12. Pour the milk-and-flour mixture on top of the egg white mixture.
13. Cook in the air fryer for 15 minutes at 330°F.

BANANA CINNAMON BREAD

Preparation Time: 10 minutes | Servings: 4

Nutrition Info (per serving)
Calories: 201 | Fat: 4 g | Protein: 5 g | Carbs: 35 g

INGREDIENTS:

- 2 bananas, mashed
- 1 large egg
- 1 cup whole-wheat flour
- 2 tablespoons honey
- 1 tablespoon butter, softened
- 1/3 cup sugar
- 1 teaspoon baking powder
- ½ teaspoon cinnamon powder
- Cooking spray

INSTRUCTIONS:

1. Combine the butter with the rest of the ingredients in a bowl and whisk thoroughly.
2. Pour the mixture into a bread or cake pan greased with cooking spray.
3. Place in your air fryer and cook at 330°F for 30 minutes.
4. Let it cool before serving.

LIVER PATE

Preparation Time: 10 minutes | Servings: 7

Nutrition Info (per serving)
Calories: 170 | Fat: 11 g | Protein: 16 g | Carbs: 3 g

INGREDIENTS:

- 1 pound chicken liver, chopped roughly
- 1 onion, peeled and diced
- 1 cup water
- 4 tablespoon butter
- 1 teaspoon salt
- 1 teaspoon ground black pepper
- ½ teaspoon dried cilantro

INSTRUCTIONS:

1. Preheat the air fryer to 360°F.
2. Place the chopped chicken liver in the air fryer basket tray.
3. Add the water and diced onion to the tray and cook the liver for 10 minutes.
4. Remove the water by straining the chicken liver and transfer to a blender.
5. Add in the butter, salt, cilantro and black pepper and blend until you get that pate texture.
6. Transfer the liver pate to a bowl and serve immediately.

Part Three

LUNCH AND DINNER RECIPES

BLACK COD WITH GRAPES AND PECAN TOPPINGS

Preparation Time: 25 minutes | Servings: 2

Nutrition Info (per serving)
Calories: 310 | Fat: 18 g | Protein: 17 g | Carbs: 12 g

INGREDIENTS:

- 2 fillets of black cod, each about 1/3 to ½ pound
- Olive oil
- Salt and ground black pepper
- 1 small bulb of fennel, sliced thinly
- 1 cup seedless grapes, halved
- ½ cup pecans
- 3 cups kale, shredded
- 2 tablespoons extra virgin olive oil
- 2 teaspoons white wine or white balsamic vinegar

INSTRUCTIONS:

1. Preheat the air fryer to 400° F.
2. Season the black cod fillets with a generous pinch each of salt and pepper.
3. Drizzle the fillets, too, with olive oil.
4. Place the fillets with their skin side down into the air fryer basket and cook for 10 minutes at 400° F.

5. Remove the cooked fillets from the air fryer, transfer to a plate, and cover loosely with a foil tent to rest.
6. In a bowl, toss the fennel, grapes and pecans; season them with salt and pepper as well as a drizzle of olive oil.
7. Place the tossed fruits and vegetable into the air fryer and cook at 400° F for 5 minutes.
8. Transfer them to a bowl and toss with the kale.
9. Dress the salad with olive oil and vinegar, season to taste with salt and pepper, and place the cooked fish fillets on top.

COLORFUL PASTA SALAD WITH ROASTED VEGETABLES

Preparation Time: 30 minutes | Servings: 6

Nutrition Info (per serving)
Calories: 341 | Fat: 5 g | Protein: 9 g | Carbs: 70 g

INGREDIENTS:

- 1 medium-sized zucchini, sliced thinly in half moons
- 1 medium-sized yellow squash, sliced in half moons
- 1 each of green, orange and red pepper, sliced in large chunks
- 1 small red onion, sliced
- ½ cup brown mushrooms, halved
- 1 teaspoon Italian seasoning
- Salt and ground black pepper to taste

- 1 pound cooked rigatoni or penne rigate pasta
- 1 cup grape tomatoes, halved
- ½ cup Kalamata olives, pitted and halved
- ¼ cup olive oil
- 3 tablespoons balsamic vinegar
- 2 tablespoons fresh basil, chopped

INSTRUCTIONS:

1. Preheat the air fryer to 380°F.
2. In a large bowl, toss the zucchini, squash, peppers, mushrooms and

red onion with olive oil. Be sure to coat the vegetables with the olive oil well but don't let them become too oily.
3. Season the vegetables with salt and pepper followed by the Italian seasoning. Toss a few times again.
4. Place the vegetables in the air fryer basket and cook for 12 minutes. Stir the basket in the 6-minute mark for even cooking. Check that the vegetables are soft, too, and extend the cooking time to 15 minutes, if necessary.
5. In a large bowl, mix well the cooked pasta, roasted vegetables, olives and tomatoes, and balsamic vinegar.
6. Season with salt and ground black pepper followed by a drizzling of olive oil for an even coating.
7. Refrigerate the salad for an hour or two before serving.
8. Serve with fresh basil on top.

PHILLY CHICKEN CHEESESTEAK STROMBOLI

Preparation Time: 45-60 minutes | Servings: 2-4

Nutrition Info (per serving)
Calories: 225 | Fat: 2 g | Protein: 9 g | Carbs: 27 g

INGREDIENTS:

- 7/8 pound pre-made pizza dough (i.e., store-bought)
- 1 ½ cup cheddar cheese, grated
- ½ cup jarred cheese sauce (e.g., Cheeze Whiz), warmed in the microwave
- 1 pound (or 2 pieces) skinless and boneless chicken breasts, thinly sliced
- ½ onion, sliced thinly
- 1 teaspoon olive oil
- 1 tablespoon Worcestershire sauce
- Salt and ground black pepper to taste

INSTRUCTIONS:

1. Preheat the air fryer to 400°F.
2. Cook the sliced onion with olive oil in the air fryer at 400°F for 8 minutes. Shake the basket at the 4-minute mark.
3. Add the chicken slices and Worcestershire sauce to the cooked sliced onions. Use a spoon to mix evenly before adding salt and black pepper to season the mix.

4. Cook for another 8 minutes at 400°F. Stir two times during the 8-minute period.
5. Remove the cooked chicken and onion from the air fryer basket, place them on a plate, and let them cool.
6. Meanwhile, roll the pizza dough on a lightly floured surface. Create a rectangular dough measuring about 11 x 13 inches; the longest side should be closest to you.
7. Sprinkle half of the grated cheddar cheese on the dough but leave a 1-inch border on the edge farthest from you empty.
8. Place the chicken and onion mixture on top of the cheese; spread it out evenly.
9. Place the remaining grated cheddar cheese and drizzle the cheese sauce on top.
10. Roll the stromboli toward the empty border starting from the side nearest you. The filling should stay tucked tightly inside the stromboli so go slowly, if necessary. Tuck the ends and pinch the seam shut when the roll is at the end of the border.
11. Make a U-shaped stromboli so that it can fit into the air fryer basket.
12. Cut 4 small slits into the top, brush it lightly with olive oil, and place it into a preheated air fryer at 370°F.
13. Cook the stromboli for 12 minutes. Be sure to invert the stromboli at the 6-minute mark.
14. Remove the cooked stromboli from the air fryer, let it rest for 2 minutes, and slice before serving.

Cooking Tip: In inverting the stromboli at its 6-minute mark, we suggest getting the basket out of the air fryer and inverting the stromboli into a plate. Then, slide the Stromboli off the plate and into the basket.

INSIDE OUT CHEESEBURGERS

Preparation Time: 30-45 minutes | Servings: 2

Nutrition Info (per serving)
Calories: 255 | Fat: 4 g | Protein: 40 g | Carbs: 17 g

INGREDIENTS:

- ¾ pound lean ground beef
- 3 tablespoons onion, minced
- 2 teaspoons yellow mustard
- 4 teaspoons ketchup
- 8 dill pickles
- 4 slices cheddar cheese, sliced into smaller pieces
- 2 burger buns
- Shredded lettuce and sliced tomato according to preference
- Salt and ground black pepper to taste

INSTRUCTIONS:

1. Combine the lean ground beef, minced onion, yellow mustard, and ketchup in a large bowl. Season with salt and pepper to taste. Mix them well.
2. Divide the beef mixture into four equal portions; use an ice cream scoop, if necessary. Flatten each beef patty.
3. On two of the beef patties, arrange 4 of the pickle chips and 2 slices

of the cheddar cheese on their center. Be sure to leave an empty space around each of the patty's edge.
4. Place the two remaining beef patties on top of the first patties. Press the two together to create beef patty sandwiches; check that the edges are sealed tightly so the stuffing will be intact inside as the burger cooks.
5. Place the beef patty sandwiches into a preheated air fryer and cook at 370°F for 20 minutes.
6. Flip the burgers at the 10-minute mark for even cooking.
7. Place the cooked cheeseburgers on buns, place lettuce and tomato on top, and serve with your favorite ketchup and sides.

CHINESE-STYLE ROASTED CAULIFLOWER WITH GENERAL TSO SAUCE

Preparation Time: 30 minutes | Servings: 4

Nutrition Info (per serving)
Calories: 390 | Fat: 10 g | Protein: 7 g | Carbs: 68 g

INGREDIENTS:

- 1 large head of cauliflower, sliced into bite-sized florets
- ¾ cup all-purpose flour
- 1 cup panko breadcrumbs
- 3 eggs
- Peanut or canola oil for spraying

For the sauce:

- ¼ cup light soy sauce
- 2 tablespoons oyster sauce
- 2 tablespoons rice wine vinegar
- 2 teaspoons chili paste
- ¼ cup water

For serving

- Steamed broccoli as a side dish
- Brown or white rice for serving

INSTRUCTIONS:

1. Preheat air fryer to 400°F.
2. In the first bowl, place the cauliflower florets and sprinkle it with ¼ cup flour. Toss the cauliflower so it's evenly coated with the flour.
3. In the second bowl, whisk the eggs.
4. In the third bowl, mix the ½ cup flour and panko breadcrumbs. This is your three-bowl dredging station.
5. Dip the florets in the beaten eggs, toss them into the flour-breadcrumbs mix, and toss to coat all sides.
6. Place the coated florets on a baking pan and spray generously them with the oil.
7. Cook the florets for 15 minutes at 400°F. Flip or turn them over after 12 minutes and spray them again with oil; continue cooking for the next 3 minutes.
8. Transfer the cooked florets to a large bowl, toss it with General Tso's sauce, and serve with rice and broccoli for a vegetarian meal.
9. Just combine the ingredients for the sauce and simmer for a minute until it thickens slightly.

SOCKEYE SALMON EN PAPILLOTTE

Preparation Time: 30-45 minutes | Servings: 2

Nutrition Info (per serving)
Calories: 75 | Fat: 3 g | Protein: 4 g | Carbs: 25 g

INGREDIENTS:

- 3 fingerling potatoes, sliced thinly in ¼-inch semicircles
- ½ bulb fennel, sliced thinly in ¼ inch strips
- 4 tablespoons unsalted butter, melted
- 2 pieces of sockeye salmon fillets, about 1/3 pound each
- ¼ cup white wine, dry vermouth, or fish stock (your choice)
- 8 cherry tomatoes, halved
- Fresh dill
- Salt and black pepper to taste

INSTRUCTIONS:

1. Preheat the air fryer to 400°F.
2. Blanch the slices of fingerling potatoes in boiling salted water for 2 minutes; boil the water on a small saucepan for this purpose. Check that the potatoes are slightly soft, not overcooked, since these will still cook in the air fryer. Drain the water and place the slices on a clean kitchen towel to dry.
3. Cut out 2 pieces of approximately 13 x 15-inch rectangles of parchment paper and set aside.

4. In a bowl, toss the blanched potatoes with the fennel, 2 tablespoons of melted butter, and salt and pepper to taste.
5. Divide the tossed vegetables between the 2 pieces of parchment paper; place them on one side of the paper only. Sprinkle fresh dill on top.
6. Place a sockeye salmon fillet on top of each vegetable pile. Season with salt and pepper again.
7. Place the halved cherry tomatoes on top.
8. Drizzle a tablespoon of melted butter and 1/8 cup of white wine/dry vermouth/fish stock on each fillet.
9. Fold the parchment square so that the fish fillet can be sealed inside it.
10. Cook the parchment-covered fish fillet in the air fryer for 10 minutes at 400°F. Depending on the capacity of your air fryer, you can either cook both at once or cook them one at a time.
11. Serve with fresh dill as garnish. You can serve it either in its parchment paper or on a plate for presentation purposes.

Cooking Tip: The fish should still feel firm to the touch when it's fully cooked. You can press through the parchment paper to do so.

GARLIC AND PARMESAN SHRIMP

Preparation Time: 15 minutes | Servings: 3-4

Nutrition Info (per serving)
Calories: 220 | Fat: 10 g | Protein: 27 g | Carbs: 5 g

INGREDIENTS:

- 2 pounds jumbo shrimp, cooked, peeled and deveined
- 2/3 cup parmesan cheese, grated
- 4 cloves garlic, minced
- 1 teaspoon basil, chopped roughly
- ½ teaspoon oregano
- 1 teaspoon ground black pepper
- 1 teaspoon onion powder
- 2 tablespoons olive oil
- 1 lemon, cut into quarters

INSTRUCTIONS:

1. In a large bowl, mix the parmesan cheese, garlic, basil, oregano, black pepper, onion powder, and olive oil. This will serve as the shrimp coating.
2. Toss the shrimp in the cheese-based coating until these are evenly coated.
3. Spray the air fryer basket with olive oil or a non-stick spray.

4. Place the tossed shrimp into the basket.
5. Cook it for 8-10 minutes at 350°F. Check that the coating on the shrimp has a golden brown appearance as it's a sign that it's ready to be served.
6. Drizzle freshly-squeezed lemon juice over the seasoned shrimp.

STUFFED CHICKEN WITH PIZZA FILLING

Preparation Time: 20 minutes | Servings: 4

Nutrition Info (per serving)
Calories: 190 | Fat: 7 g | Protein: 34 g | Carbs: 6 g

INGREDIENTS:

- 4 pieces skinless chicken breasts, deboned
- ¼ cup pre-made pizza sauce
- ½ cup cheese, shredded (Cheddar or Colby cheese)
- 16 slices of pepperoni
- 1 ½ tablespoons olive oil
- 1 ½ oregano
- Salt and pepper to taste

INSTRUCTIONS:

1. Using a rolling pin, flatten the pieces of chicken breast as thinly as possible to make fillets.
2. In a bowl, combine the pizza sauce, cheese, pepperoni, olive oil, and oregano. Season with salt and pepper and mix well.
3. Divide the pizza stuffing into four equal pieces.
4. Place the pizza stuffing into the edge of each piece of chicken breast; fill the part nearest you.
5. Roll the chicken fillet away from you. Be sure to roll as tightly as possible in a similar manner as when you're making spring rolls.

6. Secure the chicken fillet rolls with toothpicks – one at each end.
7. Cook the rolls in a preheated air fryer grill pan at 370°F for 13-15 minutes. Turn the chicken at the halfway mark of the cooking time.
8. Remove from the pan after cooking, slice and serve with vegetables, if desired.

MAC AND CHEESE

Preparation Time: 20 minutes | Servings: 2

Nutrition Info (per serving)
Calories: 320 | Fat: 13 g | Protein: 20 g | Carbs: 46 g

INGREDIENTS:

- 1 cup elbow macaroni
- ½ cup cauliflower or broccoli, cut into small florets
- ½ cup warmed milk
- 1 ½ cup cheddar cheese, grated
- 1 tablespoon parmesan cheese, grated
- Salt and pepper to taste

INSTRUCTIONS:

1. Preheat the air fryer to 350°F.
2. Cook the macaroni and cauliflower in boiling water.
3. Let it simmer for 7-10 minutes or until macaroni is al dente and cauliflower tender.
4. Drain out the water and return the macaroni and cauliflower to the pot.
5. Add the warmed milk and grated cheese to the mixture, toss well to combine, and season with salt and pepper to taste.
6. Pour the mac and cheese mixture into the air fryer's pan.

7. Sprinkle parmesan cheese on top.
8. Place the dish into the air fryer and cook for 10 minutes at 350°F.
9. Let the dish cool down in the air fryer for 5 minutes before serving.

CLASSIC STEAK AND ROASTED POTATOES

Preparation Time: 30 minutes | Servings: 1

Nutrition Info (per serving)
Calories: 239 | Fat: 5 g | Protein: 18 g | Carbs: 34 g

INGREDIENTS:

- 4 small potatoes, peeled and quartered
- 1 tablespoon olive oil
- 1 teaspoon Italian herbs
- 1 teaspoon cayenne pepper
- Salt and pepper to taste

- 1 ½ pound strip loin steak
- ½ tablespoon olive oil

INSTRUCTIONS:

1. In a bowl, mix the potatoes, olive oil, Italian herbs, and cayenne pepper. Season with salt and pepper according to your taste. Toss a few times to ensure an even coating of the seasoning on the potatoes.
2. Preheat the air fryer to 350°F for 5 minutes.
3. Place the potatoes and cook them for 16 minutes. Shake the basket at the 8-minute mark to ensure even cooking.
4. Remove the cooked potatoes from the air fryer, place them on a plate, and set aside.

5. Season the steak with olive oil, salt and pepper. Rub the seasoning on both sides of the steak, too.
6. Place the steak into the air fryer's pan and cook for 400°F for 7-12 minutes depending on your preferred doneness. The shorter the cooking time, the rarer the steak will be.
7. Once cooked, serve the steak with the roasted potatoes.

AIR FRYER-STYLE VEGETABLE GALORE

Preparation Time: 40 minutes | Servings: 4+

Nutrition Info (per serving)
Calories: 27 | Fat: 1 g | Protein: 1 g | Carbs: 3 g

INGREDIENTS:

- ½ pound carrots, peeled and sliced into 1-inch cubes
- 1 pound zucchini, cut into ¾-inch semicircles
- 1 pound yellow squash, cut into ¾-inch semicircles
- 6 tablespoons olive oil
- 1 tablespoon tarragon leaves, chopped
- Salt and pepper to taste

INSTRUCTIONS:

1. In a bowl, mix the carrots with 2 tablespoons of olive oil, as well as a pinch of salt and pepper. Toss to evenly coat the cubed carrots.
2. Place the carrots into the air fryer basket and cook for 5 minutes at 400°F.
3. In the same bowl, toss the yellow squash and zucchini with 2 tablespoons of olive oil and a pinch of salt and pepper.
4. Add the yellow squash and zucchini to the carrots.
5. Continue cooking the vegetables for 30 minutes at 400°F.
6. Shake the air fryer basket 2-3 times to ensure even cooking.

7. Remove the vegetables from the basket, place on a plate, and sprinkle tarragon leaves on top.
8. Serve with the classic steak for a complete meal.

CRISPY FRIED CHICKEN WITH ROASTED VEGGIES

Preparation Time: 30 minutes | Servings: 4

Nutrition Info (per serving)
Calories: 527 | Fat: 32 g | Protein: 48 g | Carbs: 40 g

INGREDIENTS:

- 8 chicken thighs
- ¾ cup mushrooms, sliced
- 1 red onion, diced
- ½ cup carrots, cut into 1-inch cubes
- 2 red bell peppers, deseeded and diced
- 10 medium asparagus
- 2 tablespoons extra-virgin olive oil
- ¼ cup balsamic vinegar
- ½ teaspoon sugar
- ½ tablespoon dried oregano
- 1 ½ tablespoon fresh rosemary
- 2 cloves garlic, chopped finely
- Salt and ground black pepper to taste
- Fresh sage, chopped finely

INSTRUCTIONS:

1. Preheat the air fryer to 400°F.
2. Grease the air fryer's pan with olive oil.

3. On a plate, rub the chicken thighs with salt and pepper. Don't overdo on the seasoning since there will be other flavors added to the fried chicken.
4. In a large bowl, mix all the vegetables (mushrooms, onion, carrots, bell peppers, and asparagus), the herbs (oregano, rosemary, and garlic), and the dressing (balsamic vinegar and sugar mixed). Toss until the vegetables are evenly coated.
5. Arrange the vegetables on the greased baking tray.
6. Arrange the chicken thighs on top of the vegetables.
7. Place the pan into the cooking chamber and roast for 20 minutes.
8. Serve with fresh sage once cooked.

GLUTEN-FREE SALMON CROQUETTES

Preparation Time: 20 minutes | Servings: 2

Nutrition Info (per serving)
Calories: 503 | Fat: 33 g | Protein: 21 g | Carbs: 32 g

INGREDIENTS:

- 1 large tin canned red salmon, about 1 pound drained of its liquid
- 2 medium-sized eggs, whisked lightly
- ½ bunch fresh parsley, chopped roughly
- ½ cup vegetable or olive oil of your choice
- ½ cup gluten-free rice crumbs (or regular if you don't mind gluten)
- Salt and pepper to taste

INSTRUCTIONS:

1. Preheat the air fryer to 400°F.
2. In a bowl, mash the salmon with a fork but keep it relatively chunky.
3. Mix the eggs and parsley with the salmon. Season with salt and pepper.
4. In another bowl, mix the olive oil and rice crumbs until a loose mixture forms.
5. Make salmon balls, about 16 pieces, using your hands.
6. Coat the salmon balls in the rice crumbs mixture.
7. Cook them in the air fryer for 7 minutes at 400°F or until the croquettes are golden brown in color.

CLASSIC ROAST CHICKEN

Preparation Time: 60 minutes | Servings: 4-6

Nutrition Info (per serving)
Calories: 146 | Fat: 4 g | Protein: 29 g | Carbs: 1 g

INGREDIENTS:

- 5-pound whole chicken, approximate

Dry Rub:

- ¾ cup kosher salt
- ¼ cup onion powder
- ¼ cup paprika
- ¼ cup garlic powder
- ¼ cup Italian seasoning
- ¼ cup brown sugar
- 2 tablespoons cayenne pepper
- 2 tablespoons dried thyme
- 2 tablespoons dry mustard
- 2 tablespoons garlic pepper

INSTRUCTIONS:

1. Preheat the air fryer to 330°F.
2. Wash the chicken and pat dry with a clean kitchen towel. Tie the legs

CLASSIC ROAST CHICKEN

and wings so that the chicken will not spread apart during the cooking process.
3. In a bowl, combine all the ingredients for the dry rub.
4. Sprinkle the dry rub on the chicken. Use your hands to rub the seasoning on every part of the chicken, especially around the joints of the legs and wings.
5. Spray the air fryer's basket with cooking spray.
6. Place the chicken into the basket with its legs facing down.
7. Roast the chicken for 30 minutes at 330°F.
8. Flip the chicken so its legs are facing up and continue cooking for another 20 minutes.
9. Check the chicken's internal temperature using a meat thermometer. If it's already 165°F, then it's already cooked and ready to serve with roasted vegetables.

CHINESE SWEET AND SOUR PORK

Preparation Time: 30 minutes | Servings: 4

Nutrition Info (per serving)
Calories: 335 | Fat: 10 g | Protein: 27 g | Carbs: 36 g

INGREDIENTS:

- 2 pounds pork, cut into 1-inch chunks
- 2 large eggs
- 1 cup cornstarch or potato starch
- 1/16 teaspoon Chinese five-spice
- 3 tablespoons canola oil
- 1 teaspoon pure sesame oil
- Sea salt and pepper to taste

For the sweet and sour sauce:

- ½ cup sugar
- ½ cup seasoned rice vinegar
- 5 tablespoons ketchup
- 1 tablespoon light soy sauce
- ¼ teaspoon sea salt
- ½ teaspoon garlic powder

INSTRUCTIONS:

1. To make the sweet and sour sauce, combine the ingredients in a bowl and stir a few times. Pour the mixture into a skillet placed over medium high heat and whisk the ingredients for about 5 minutes. Turn the heat to its lowest setting and let the mixture simmer, uncovered, for another 5 minutes.
2. To set up a dredging station, get two bowls. In the first bowl, mix the potato starch or cornstarch, Chinese five-spice seasoning, and season with salt and pepper to taste. In the second bowl, beat the eggs with the sesame oil.
3. Dredge the pork cubes into the starch coating mix and shake off the excess. Dip them into the egg mixture, shake off the excess, and then re-dip into the starch coating mix.
4. Coat or spray the air fryer basket with the canola oil.
5. Place the pork cubes into the basket and spray them with canola oil.
6. Cook the pork cubes at 340°F for 8-12 minutes or until the meat is cooked through. Shake the basket twice during the cooking process for even cooking.
7. Serve with the sweet and sour sauce drizzled on top.

KABAB KOOBIDEH

Preparation Time: 30 minutes | Servings: 3-4

Nutrition Info (per serving)
Calories: 470 | Fat: 37 g | Protein: 43 g | Carbs: 7 g

INGREDIENTS:

- 1 pound chicken breasts and thighs, deboned
- 3 cloves garlic
- 1 large onion, chopped
- 2 tomatoes, sliced
- 1 large egg
- ¼ cup flat leaf parsley
- ½ cup plan breadcrumbs
- 1 teaspoon lemon juice
- ¼ teaspoon turmeric powder
- ½ teaspoon ground black pepper

INSTRUCTIONS:

1. Place the chopped onion into a paper towel, roll it up, and squeeze the excess water out of the onion. Repeat the process in another paper towel.
2. In a food processor, combine the chicken, garlic, onion, half of the breadcrumbs, egg, parsley, turmeric, lemon juice, and salt and

pepper. Mix well for a minute or two until the ingredients are fully combined. Add more breadcrumbs in case the mixture is still wet.
3. Chill the chicken mixture in the freezer for 15 minutes.
4. Divide the chicken mixture into six equal portions and roll each portion around a skewer, about 6 inches long.
5. Grease the air fryer basket with oil and place the 6 kabobs into it. Spray the kabobs again. (For a smaller air fryer, you may have to cook the kabobs in batches)
6. Cook the kabobs at 400°F for 6 minutes.
7. After 6 minutes, flip the kabobs and add the sliced tomatoes on top.
8. Spray the food with olive oil again and cook for another 5 minutes or until the tomatoes are soft.
9. Serve the cooked kabob and tomatoes over basmati rice, drizzle with fresh lemon juice, and sprinkle sumac on top.

Cooking Tip: Substitute the chicken with ground beef, lamb, or turkey, if you want.

CHEESY CHICKEN PARMESAN

Preparation Time: 30 Minutes | Servings: 2

Nutrition Info (per serving)
Calories: 415 | Fat: 14 g | Protein: 33 g | Carbs: 33 g

INGREDIENTS:

- 2 pieces of fat-trimmed chicken breast, about ½ pound each, halved
- 1 cup breadcrumbs
- 6 tablespoons parmesan cheese, grated
- 1 tablespoon melted butter or olive oil
- 6 tablespoon mozzarella cheese, preferably with reduced fat
- ½ cup marinara sauce
- Cooking spray

INSTRUCTIONS:

1. Preheat the air fryer to 360°F for 10 minutes.
2. In a bowl, mix the breadcrumbs and parmesan cheese.
3. Brush the melted butter or olive oil on the chicken pieces and dip them into the cheese-breadcrumbs mixture.
4. Spray the air fryer basket with cooking spray, place the chicken pieces into it, and spray the chicken with oil again.
5. Cook the chicken pieces for 6 minutes at 360°F. Do this in two batches for smaller air fryers.

6. Turn the chicken pieces, top with mozzarella cheese and marinara sauce.
7. Cook for 3 more minutes or until the cheese has melted.

TIJUANA-STYLE STREET TACO

Preparation Time: 30 minutes excluding chilling time | Servings: 3-4

Nutrition Info (per serving)
Calories: 320 | Fat: 17 g | Protein: 18 | Carbs: 22 g

INGREDIENTS:

- 2 pounds sirloin tips, sliced
- 4 cloves garlic, minced finely
- 2 teaspoons kosher salt
- 2 tablespoons muscovado sugar, divided into two parts
- 1 ½ teaspoons ground cumin
- 1 ½ teaspoons dried oregano
- 1 ½ teaspoons ground annatto seeds
- 1 teaspoon chipotle peppers in adobo sauce (bought from supermarket)
- 1 can pineapple slices with the juice drained and set aside in a bowl
- 10 flour or corn tortillas
- Pico de gallo for garnishing
- Fresh lime, cut into wedges

INSTRUCTIONS:

1. In a large bowl, mix the sirloin tips, chipotle, cumin, oregano, annatto seeds, and ¼ cup pineapple juice. Season with the salt and 1

tablespoon muscovado sugar. Check that the meat is evenly coated with the seasoning. Cover and refrigerate for 45-60 minutes.
2. Preheat the air fryer to 400°F for 5 minutes. Pull out the basket afterwards and mist with a light spray of cooking oil.
3. Place the seasoned meat into the air fryer basket, place the pineapple slices on top, and sprinkle the remaining muscovado sugar on top.
4. Cook the seasoned meat at 390°F for 8 minutes.
5. Remove the cooked meat from the basket and serve on top of tortillas. Top with pico de gallo and garnish with a lime wedge.

CRISPY NOODLE SALAD

Preparation Time: 40 minutes | Servings: 2

Nutrition Info (per serving)
Calories: 130 | Fat: 8 g | Protein: 3 g | Carbs: 9 g

INGREDIENTS:

- 1 package wheat noodles
- 1 tablespoon olive oil
- 1 tablespoon tamari
- 1 tablespoon lime juice
- 1 tablespoon red chili sauce
- 1 onion, julienned
- 1 cup cabbage, julienned
- 1 green bell pepper, julienned
- 1 carrot, julienned
- 1 sprig coriander, chopped roughly
- 1 tomato, sliced
- Salt and pepper to taste

INSTRUCTIONS:

1. Preheat the air fryer at 395°F for 5 minutes.
2. Cook the noodles in boiling water until these are half-cooked only. Pour the half-cooked noodles into a colander to drain.

3. Pour the noodles into a bowl, pour oil over the noodles, and mix the two until the noodles are evenly coated.
4. Place tin foil on the air fryer basket's base and place the noodles in it.
5. Cook the noodles for 15-20 minutes at 395°F. The noodles should be crisp when taken out of the basket.
6. Meanwhile, mix the red chili sauce, tamari, and lime juice in a small bowl. Season with salt and pepper.
7. In a large bowl, mix the vegetables – onion, cabbage, bell pepper, carrot, tomato, and coriander. Add the noodles and drizzle with olive oil before serving.

FLOURLESS CHICKEN CORDON BLEU

Preparation Time: 30 minutes | Servings: 2

Nutrition Info (per serving)
Calories: 165 | Fat: 7 g | Protein: 26 g | Carbs: 3 g

INGREDIENTS:

- 2 pieces chicken breasts, boneless and skinless
- 1 tablespoon soft cheese
- 1 teaspoon parsley
- 1 slice cheddar cheese, sliced in two
- 1 sliced ham, sliced in two
- 1 large egg, whisked
- 2 ¼ tablespoons oats
- 1 teaspoon garlic puree
- 1 tablespoon thyme
- 1 tablespoon tarragon
- Salt and pepper to taste

INSTRUCTIONS:

1. Preheat the air fryer to 400°F for 5 minutes.
2. Chop the chicken breasts at a side angle to the corner. You should be able to add the stuffing at the center and fold the chicken breasts over.

3. Season the chicken with salt, pepper and tarragon. Be sure to season all sides for more flavor.
4. In a bowl, mix the garlic, soft cheese, and parsley to make the cheese mixture. Stir to mix well.
5. Spread a layer of the cheese mixture in the center of the chicken breast and place a slice of ham and cheese on top.
6. Fold and press down on the stuffed chicken breast to seal it.
7. Set up a dredging station – one bowl holds the beaten egg and another bowl holds the oats with the thyme and tarragon.
8. Dip the chicken breast roll in the oats mixture first, then in the egg, and back to the oats mixture.
9. Place the coated chicken breast rolls on a baking sheet in the air fryer and cook them at 400°F for 30 minutes. After 20 minutes of cooking time, flip them over so that both sides will be crispy.
10. Serve with roasted potatoes.

Cooking Tip: Add more cheese for a cheesier chicken cordon bleu.

ROASTED STUFFED PEPPERS

Preparation Time: 45 minutes | Servings: 2

Nutrition Info (per serving)
Calories: 175 | Fat: 10 g | Protein: 7 g | Carbs: 9 g

INGREDIENTS:

- 2 large green bell peppers
- ½ pound lean ground beef
- 1 small onion, diced
- 1 clove garlic, minced
- 1 teaspoon olive oil
- ½ cup tomato sauce
- 1 teaspoon Worcestershire sauce
- ½ cup cheddar cheese, grated
- Salt and pepper to taste (½ teaspoon each is usually sufficient)

INSTRUCTIONS

1. Make a hole in the center of each green bell pepper's stem; remove the stem and seeds, too. Cook them in boiling salted water for 2-3 minutes, drain the water, and set aside.
2. In a skillet, pour the olive oil and sauté the onion and garlic until translucent and golden brown, respectively. Remove the skillet from the heat and let them cool.
3. In a bowl, mix the ground beef, sautéed onion and garlic,

Worcestershire sauce, half of the tomato sauce, and half of the shredded cheese. Season with salt and pepper. Be sure to mix well for well-seasoned meat.
4. Fill the green bell pepper with the meat stuffing until ¾ of the way only. Fill the top with the remaining cheese and tomato sauce.
5. Spray the air fryer basket with olive oil and preheat at 390°F.
6. Place the stuffed green bell peppers into the air fryer and cook at 390°F for 15-20 minutes.

TURKEY BREAST WITH MAPLE MUSTARD GLAZE

Preparation Time: 70 minutes | Serves: 6-8

Nutrition Info (per serving)
Calories: 170 | Fat: 9 g | Protein: 13 g | Carbs: 10 g

INGREDIENTS:

- 1 whole turkey breast, about 5 pounds
- 1 tablespoon olive oil
- ½ teaspoon smoked paprika
- 1 teaspoon dried thyme
- ½ teaspoons dried sage
- ½ teaspoon black pepper
- 1 teaspoon salt
- ¼ cup maple syrup
- 1 tablespoon Dijon mustard
- 1 tablespoon unsalted butter, melted

INSTRUCTIONS:

1. Preheat the air fryer to 350°F.
2. Brush the turkey breast with olive oil. Better yet, massage the olive oil into the breast using your hands.
3. In a bowl, mix the thyme, sage and paprika, as well as the salt and pepper. When the spices have been mixed well, rub the dry mix on the turkey breast. Be sure to cover the meat on all sides.

4. Cook the turkey breast at 350°F for 25 minutes.
5. Turn it on its other side and cook for another 12 minutes.
6. Turn it again and cook for 12 minutes again.
7. Check its internal temperature by using a meat thermometer; the meat should be 165°F after the 50-minute cooking time.
8. In a saucepan, mix the mustard, maple syrup, and melted butter. The mixture should be smooth after a few stirs.
9. Cover the cooked turkey breast with the maple syrup and cook it again in the air fryer for 5 minutes at 350°F.
10. Remove the turkey breast from the air fryer, place it on a plate, and cover with aluminum foil.
11. Let it rest for 5 minutes before slicing and serving.

Cooking Tip # 1: Trim the bottom part of the turkey breast (i.e., ribs), if it's too large for the air fryer. The meat should sit upright in the basket for even cooking without being in direct contact with the heating element.

Cooking Tip # 2: Make another glaze by combining ½ cup cherry preserves, 1 teaspoon soy sauce, and 1 tablespoon chopped thyme leaves. Season with salt and pepper, too.

CRISPY ROAST PORK

Preparation Time: 5 hours (4 hours for preparation including drying time, 1 hour for air frying) | Servings: 2-4

Nutrition Info (per serving)
Calories: 212 | Fat: 16 g | Protein: 13 g | Carbs: 5 g

INGREDIENTS:

- 1 ½ pounds pork belly

Dry Rub:

- 2 teaspoons garlic salt
- 1 teaspoon five spice powder
- 1 teaspoon ground white pepper

- Lemon juice

INSTRUCTIONS:

1. Wash the pork belly, pluck the excess hair and trim the excess fat, and pat dry.
2. Cook it in boiling water until cooked through. This should take about an hour but you can also determine doneness by using the knife test.
3. Remove it from the water afterwards and let it air-dry in the open.

This should take 3 to 4 hours during which time you can make the accompaniment to the crispy roast pork, such as air-fried roasted vegetables. This should also provide an opportunity to pluck excess hair from its skin.

4. Pat dry with a kitchen towel to remove any excess water from the pork belly.
5. Prick it with a sharp skewer in as many places as possible – the more holes, the crispier the skin.
6. Score the skin, too, with a knife but do it lightly.
7. Massage the dry rub on the pork belly's meat area only.
8. Rub lemon juice and followed by sea salt on the skin.
9. Preheat the air fryer to 320°F for 5 minutes.
10. Place the pork belly with its meat side facing down and its skin facing up into the air fryer.
11. Cook it for 30 minutes at 320°F and then at 356°F for another 30 minutes.

STICKY MUSHROOM RICE

Preparation Time: 30 minutes | Servings: 6

Nutrition Info (per serving)
Calories: 442 | Fat: 7 g | Protein: 10 g | Carbs: 87 g

INGREDIENTS:

- 1 pound jasmine rice, cooked

- ½ cup soy sauce
- 4 cloves garlic, minced
- 4 tablespoons maple syrup
- 2 teaspoon Chinese five spice
- ½ teaspoon powdered ginger
- 4 tablespoons white wine

- 1 pound cleaned cremini mushrooms, whole (Cut in half in case of larger mushrooms)
- ½ cup frozen peas

INSTRUCTIONS:

1. Mix the 6 ingredients for the sauce – soy sauce, garlic, maple syrup, five spice, ginger, and white wine – in a bowl. Set aside.
2. Cook the mushrooms in the air fryer at 350°F for 10 minutes.

3. Stir the mushrooms after 10 minutes.
4. Pour the sauce and peas over the mushroom, stir a couple of times, and cook for 5 minutes again.
5. Pour the mushrooms over the cooked jasmine rice and serve with your choice in meat.

CAJUN-STYLE SALMON

Preparation Time: 15 minutes | Servings: 2

Nutrition Info (per serving)
Calories: 164 | Fat: 8 g | Protein: 20 g | Carbs: 1 g

INGREDIENTS:

- 2 pieces of fresh salmon fillet, each about ½ pound
- 1 tablespoon Cajun seasoning
- 1 lemon, quartered, for serving

INSTRUCTIONS:

1. Preheat the air fryer to 350°F for 5 minutes.
2. Wash the salmon fillets, pat dry with a clean kitchen towel, and place them on a plate.
3. Sprinkle with the Cajun seasoning and coat all sides. For added sweetness, if desired, give the fillets a light sprinkling of sugar, too.
4. Cook the fillets at 350°F for 7-8 minutes depending on their thickness. The skin should be facing up when placed in the air fryer's pan.
5. Serve with a wedge of lemon.

3. Stir the mushrooms after 10 minutes.
4. Pour the sauce and peas over the mushroom, stir a couple of times, and cook for 5 minutes again.
5. Pour the mushrooms over the cooked jasmine rice and serve with your choice in meat.

CAJUN-STYLE SALMON

Preparation Time: 15 minutes | Servings: 2

Nutrition Info (per serving)
Calories: 164 | Fat: 8 g | Protein: 20 g | Carbs: 1 g

INGREDIENTS:

- 2 pieces of fresh salmon fillet, each about ½ pound
- 1 tablespoon Cajun seasoning
- 1 lemon, quartered, for serving

INSTRUCTIONS:

1. Preheat the air fryer to 350°F for 5 minutes.
2. Wash the salmon fillets, pat dry with a clean kitchen towel, and place them on a plate.
3. Sprinkle with the Cajun seasoning and coat all sides. For added sweetness, if desired, give the fillets a light sprinkling of sugar, too.
4. Cook the fillets at 350°F for 7-8 minutes depending on their thickness. The skin should be facing up when placed in the air fryer's pan.
5. Serve with a wedge of lemon.

BANG BANG FRIED SHRIMP

Preparation Time: 30 minutes | Servings: 4

Nutrition Info (per serving)
Calories: 330 | Fat: 15 g | Protein: 25 g | Carbs: 26 g

INGREDIENTS:

- 1 pound raw shrimp, peeled and deveined
- 1 teaspoon paprika
- Salt and pepper to taste

- 1 egg white
- ½ cup all-purpose flour
- ¾ cup panko breadcrumbs
- Cooking spray

For the sauce: (Mix thoroughly to combine)

- 1/3 cup plain Greek yogurt
- 2 tablespoon Sriracha
- ¼ cup sweet chili sauce

INSTRUCTIONS:

1. Preheat the air fryer to 400°F.

2. Meanwhile, season the shrimp with the paprika, salt and pepper mix. Toss well for an even coating.
3. Set up a dredging station by placing the egg white, all-purpose flour, and panko breadcrumbs in three separate bowls.
4. Dip the shrimp in flour, followed by dipping in the egg whites, and finally in the panko breadcrumbs.
5. Spray the coated shrimp with cooking spray.
6. Place the shrimp in the air fryer basket and cook for 4 minutes at 400°F.
7. Flip the shrimp to the other side and cook for another 4 minutes at 400°F. The shrimp should be crisp.
8. Serve with the sauce drizzled on top.

BAKED GARLIC PARSLEY POTATOES

Preparation Time: 40 minutes | Servings: 3

Nutrition Info (per serving)
Calories: 65 | Fat: 1 g | Protein: 2 g | Carbs: 12 g

INGREDIENTS:

- 3 Russet or Idaho baking potatoes, whole
- 2 tablespoons olive oil
- 1 tablespoon garlic
- 1 teaspoon parsley
- 1 tablespoon salt

INSTRUCTIONS:

1. Wash the potatoes, pat dry with a kitchen towel, and poke air holes in them; use a fork.
2. Coat the potatoes with the mixture of olive oil, garlic, parsley, and salt.
3. Place in the air fryer basket and cook them at 392°F for 35 minutes.
4. Serve with your favorite dressing, such as sour cream and fresh parsley, perhaps with salt and pepper pork chops.

SALT AND PEPPER PORK CHOPS

Preparation Time: 30 minutes | Servings: 4

Nutrition Info (per serving)
Calories: 370 | Fat: 28 g | Protein: 46 g | Carbs: 3 g

INGREDIENTS:

- 6 pieces pork chops, cut into cutlet (bite-sized) pieces
- 2 egg whites
- ½ teaspoon salt
- ¼ teaspoon black pepper
- 1 cup cornstarch or potato starch

For the stir fried vegetables:

- 2 pieces jalapeno pepper, deseeded and sliced
- 2 green onions, trimmed and sliced
- 2 tablespoons peanut or canola oil
- Salt and pepper to taste

INSTRUCTIONS:

1. Spray the air fryer basket with oil and preheat at 360°F for 5 minutes.
2. In a bowl, whisk the egg white until foamy. Be sure to season with salt and pepper.

SALT AND PEPPER PORK CHOPS

3. Add the pork cutlets to the egg white mixture and marinate for 15 minutes.
4. Add the cornstarch or potato starch into the pork cutlets marinated in the egg white mixture. Toss with your hands or with a spoon until thoroughly mixed.
5. Shake off the excess cornstarch and place the pork cutlets into the preheated air fryer basket.
6. Lightly spray the pork cutlets' surface with oil.
7. Cook them at 360°F for 12 minutes. Shake the basket and spray the pork cutlets with oil twice during the cooking process.
8. Cook for another 6 minutes at 400°F or until the pork cutlets have a crispy texture and golden color.

For the stir fry:

1. Heat a wok or skillet until it's smoking hot.
2. Place the oil into the hot skillet.
3. Place the scallions, jalapeno peppers, salt and pepper into the oil and stir fry them for a minute. Stir or toss a few times to avoid burning the vegetables.
4. Add the air-fried pork cutlets to the vegetable mix and cook for another minute.
5. Serve hot.

RAVIOLI WITH MARINARA SAUCE

Preparation Time: 10 minutes | Servings: 6

Nutrition Info (per serving)
Calories: 338 | Fat: 13 g | Protein: 21 g | Carbs: 34 g

INGREDIENTS:

- 1 jar of 14-ounce premade marinara sauce
- 1 box of 9-ounce ready-to-cook cheese or meat ravioli
- 1 teaspoon olive oil
- 1 cups Italian-style breadcrumbs
- 1 cup buttermilk
- ¼ cup Parmesan cheese

INSTRUCTIONS:

1. Preheat the air fryer to 200°F.
2. In a bowl, pour the buttermilk and dip the ravioli in it.
3. In another bowl, combine the breadcrumbs and olive. Stir a few times to mix well.
4. Press the buttermilk-coated ravioli into the breadcrumbs-olive mixture.
5. Place baking paper on the air fryer basket and place the breaded ravioli on top.
6. Cook the ravioli for 5 minutes at 200°F.
7. Serve the cooked ravioli with the marinara sauce for dipping.

MUSHROOM CHICKEN BROCCOLI CASSEROLE

Preparation Time: 30 minutes | Servings: 4

Nutrition Info (per serving)
Calories: 256 | Fat: 6 g | Protein: 28 g | Carbs: 24 g

INGREDIENTS:

- 4 pieces chicken breast, cut into cubes
- 1 cup coconut milk
- 1 cup mushrooms
- ½ cup cheese, grated
- 1 small broccoli, cut into florets
- 1 tablespoon curry powder
- Salt to taste

INSTRUCTIONS:

1. Preheat the air fryer to 350°F.
2. In a bowl, mix the coconut milk and curry powder, as well as season with a pinch of salt.
3. Add the chicken, mushroom, and broccoli. Stir a few times to combine well.
4. Pour the chicken mixture into the air fryer pan and cook for 20 minutes at 350°F.

Part Four
DESSERT RECIPES

MINI STRAWBERRY ROLLS

Preparation Time: 25 minutes | Servings: 8

Nutrition Info (per serving)
Calories: 81 | Fat: 2 g | Protein: 1 g | Carbs: 18 g

INGREDIENTS:

- ½ cup powdered sugar
- 1/8 teaspoon cinnamon powder
- ¼ teaspoon ground cloves
- 1 teaspoon vanilla extract
- 1 can of 12-ounce biscuit dough
- ¼ cup butter, melted
- 12 ounces ready-made strawberry pie filling

INSTRUCTIONS:

1. In a bowl, mix well the powdered sugar, cinnamon powder, ground cloves, and vanilla extract to make the spiced sugar mixture.
2. On a lightly floured surface, stretch and flatten each piece of the ready-made biscuit dough until a round dough is created. Use a rolling pin for best results.
3. In the center of each round biscuit dough, place an equal amount of the strawberry pie filling.
4. Roll the biscuit dough like a spring roll and seal the ends; fold and press at the ends.

5. Dip the pieces into the melted butter.
6. Cover the pieces with the spiced sugar mixture and then spray them lightly with a non-stick coating on all sides.
7. Bake the pies at 340°F for 10-12 minutes or until golden brown.
8. Remove from the air fryer and let them cool for 5 minutes before serving. The pies can be served with whipped cream on top or the side for more creaminess.

APPLE DUMPLINGS

Preparation Time: 35 minutes | Servings: 2

Nutrition Info (per serving)
Calories: 288 | Fat: 12 g | Protein: 2 g | Carbs: 41 g

INGREDIENTS:

- 2 small apples, peeled and cored
- 2 tablespoons raisins
- 2 sheets puff pastry
- 1 tablespoon muscovado sugar (or brown sugar)
- 1 tablespoon butter, melted

INSTRUCTIONS:

1. Preheat the air fryer to 356°F for 5 minutes.
2. In a bowl, mix the raisins and muscovado sugar to make the filling.
3. Place each apple on its own puff pastry sheet, fill its core with the filling, and completely cover the apple with the puff pastry sheet. Just fold over the edges of the sheet over the apple to do so.
4. Brush the dough with the melted butter.
5. Place a small sheet of foil in the air fryer's cooking chamber to catch excess juices from the apple dumplings.
6. Place the apple dumplings on top of the foil.
7. Bake the apple dumplings for 25 minutes at 356°F or until these are golden brown in color. The apples should be soft, too.

8. At the halfway mark (about 13 minutes) of the cooking time, turn the apple dumplings once to ensure even cooking.
9. Remove from the air fryer, let them cool for 10 minutes, and serve with vanilla ice cream.

Cooking Tip: Keep the shape of the apples intact with just a hole for the raisin-muscovado filling; the hole will be created when the apples' cores have been removed. Choose the smallest possible apple that will fit into a single puff pastry sheet.

CHOCOLATE CHIP COOKIES

Preparation Time: 15 minutes | Servings: 8

Nutrition Info (per serving)
Calories: 266 | Fat: 14 g | Protein: 4 g | Carbs: 39 g

INGREDIENTS:

- 7/8 cup self-rising flour
- 3 ½ ounce butter, softened
- 6 tablespoons brown sugar
- 3 ½ ounce chocolate bar
- 1 tablespoon milk
- 2 tablespoon honey

INSTRUCTIONS:

1. Preheat the air fryer to 356°F.
2. Place the chocolate bar in a plastic bag and smash it using a rolling pin. The result should be a mix of chunky and fine chunks. Set aside.
3. In a bowl, beat the butter until soft enough to incorporate the sugar. Cream the two ingredients together until a light and fluffy mixture is created.
4. Add the flour and honey to the butter-sugar mixture. Don't overdo the mixing to prevent a stiff dough.
5. Add the chocolate and milk to the dough and fold them into it. The chocolate chunks should be evenly distributed as much as possible.

6. Place a baking sheet in the pan to prevent the cookies from sticking to the bottom.
7. Using a small ice cream scooper, make small balls of dough and place them in the air fryer's baking sheet-covered pan.
8. Bake the cookies at 356°F for 6 minutes.
9. Decrease the temperature to 320°F and bake for 2 minutes more.
10. Remove from the air fryer and let the cookies cool on a rack for 5 minutes before serving.

NUTELLA BANANA SANDWICH

Preparation Time: 15 minutes | Servings: 2

Nutrition Info (per serving)
Calories: 65 | Fat: 2 g | Protein: 2 g | Carbs: 11 g

INGREDIENTS:

- 4 slices white bread
- 1 bar butter, softened
- ¼ cup Nutella or any chocolate hazelnut spread of your choice
- 1 large banana

INSTRUCTIONS:

1. Preheat the air fryer to 370°F.
2. Spread softened butter on all the 4 bread slices.
3. Place the buttered slices with their buttered side down on a clean plate or counter.
4. Spread Nutella on the other side of the bread slices and set aside.
5. Cut the banana in half (i.e., crosswise) and slice each half into 3 slices (i.e., lengthwise).
6. To make a sandwich, place 3 sliced bananas on top of a slice of bread and then top with the other slice. You should get 2 sandwiches.
7. Cut each sandwich in half, either triangle or rectangular depending on the size of the air fryer.
8. Place the sandwiches in the air fryer and cook for 5 minutes at 370°F.

9. Flip the sandwiches and cook for another 2 minutes at 370°F or until the sandwiches have a golden color.
10. Remove from the air fryer, let them cool, and serve with a glass of milk, orange juice, or black coffee.

Cooking Tip: Substitute other fruits for the bananas, such as strawberries, peaches, and raspberries.

FRUIT CRUMBLE MUG CAKES

Preparation Time: 30 minutes | Servings: 4

Nutrition Info (per serving)
Calories: 247 | Fat: 11 g | Protein: 5 g | Carbs: 54 g

INGREDIENTS:

- 1 cup all-purpose flour
- 1 ¾ ounce butter
- 2 tablespoons caster sugar
- 2 tablespoons oats
- 5 teaspoons muscovado or brown sugar
- 1 small apple
- 1 small peach
- 1 small pear
- 4 plums
- ½ cup blueberries
- 1 tablespoon honey

INSTRUCTIONS:

1. Preheat the air fryer to 320°F.
2. Remove the stones and cores from the fruits (apple, peach, and pear).
3. Cut them into small cubes and combine in a bowl. Add the blueberries. Mix well for even distribution.
4. Divide the mixed fruits into four portions.

5. Place an equal amount of the mixed fruits in 4 oven-safe mugs. Check that the mugs will fit into the air fryer's cooking chamber.
6. In a mixing bowl, combine the all-purpose flour, caster sugar, and butter. Mix these ingredients until the mixture resembles fine breadcrumbs (i.e., crumble).
7. Add the oats to the dough and incorporate well to form the final crumble.
8. Divide the crumble into four portions.
9. Cover the top of each mug with a single layer of crumble.
10. Place the mugs in the air fryer and bake at 320°F for 10 minutes.
11. Increase the heat to 392°F and bake for another 5 minutes.
12. Remove from the air fryer and let the cakes cool for 5-10 minutes before serving.

BLONDIE AND BROWNIE BARS

Preparation Time: 30-45 minutes | Servings: 15-20 bars

Nutrition Info (per serving)
Calories: 457 | Fat: 35 g | Protein: 6 g | Carbs: 62 g

INGREDIENTS:

- 1 pound pre-made chocolate chip cookie dough (Buy one from a store for convenience)
- 1 egg
- ½ cup sugar
- ¼ cup vegetable oil
- ¼ cup cocoa powder
- ¼ cup all-purpose flour
- ⅛ teaspoon baking powder
- ⅛ teaspoon salt

INSTRUCTIONS:

1. Preheat the air fryer to 350°F.
2. Line a 7-inch baking pan, which should fit into the air fryer's cooking chamber, with either aluminum foil or parchment paper. Spray both the baking pan and the parchment/foil with oil or grease them with butter.
3. Press the premade cookie dough into the cake pan using your

fingers; check for even layer. Transfer the pan with its cookie dough to the air fryer basket.
4. Bake the cookie dough, without a cover, for 8 minutes at 350°F. This will be the cookie layer.
5. Meanwhile, make the brownie batter by combining the eggs, sugar and oil (i.e., wet ingredients) in a bowl.
6. In another bowl, mix the all-purpose flour, cocoa powder, baking powder, and salt (i.e., dry ingredients).
7. Gradually add the dry ingredients to the wet ingredients. Stir until the two mixtures are combined well but avoid over-mixing. This will be the brownie batter.
8. Pour the brownie batter on top of the cookie layer. Use a spatula to even out the brownie layer.
9. Bake the bars again, without a cover, for 15 minutes at 350°F.
10. Transfer the cake pan to a cooling rack and let the cake cool for 10 minutes.
11. Cut the cake into square or rectangular bars.
12. Serve with vanilla ice cream, if desired.

BANANA-VANILLA PASTRY PUFFS

Preparation Time: 20 minutes | Servings: 8

Nutrition Info (per serving)
Calories: 377 | Fat: 26 g | Protein: 8 g | Carbs: 30 g

INGREDIENTS:

- ½ pound (1 pack) crescent dinner rolls (Keep refrigerated before cooking)
- 1 cup milk
- 4 ounces instant vanilla pudding
- 4 ounces cream cheese, softened
- 2 ripe bananas, peeled and sliced in circles
- 1 egg, lightly whisked

INSTRUCTIONS:

1. Unroll the crescent dinner rolls and cut into 8 squares.
2. Mix the pudding and milk well using a whisk.
3. Add the cream cheese and whisk until a smooth pudding mixture forms.
4. Place an equal amount of pudding mixture into the center of each pastry square.
5. Top with a few slices of the banana.
6. Fold the pastry square over the pudding-banana filling and press the edges to seal it.

7. Brush each of the pastry squares with the whisked egg; it will give the surface a delectable gloss.
8. Bake the pastry at 355°F for 10 minutes.

EASY CHOCOLATE SOUFFLÉS

Preparation Time: 30 minutes | Servings: 2

Nutrition Info (per serving)
Calories: # | Fat: # g | Protein: # g | Carbs: # g

INGREDIENTS:

- 3 ounces semi-sweet chocolate, chopped into chunks
- ¼ cup butter
- 2 eggs, separate the yolk from the white and set aside in two bowls
- 2 tablespoons all-purpose flour
- 3 tablespoons sugar
- ½ teaspoon vanilla extract
- Powdered sugar and heavy cream as garnish

INSTRUCTIONS:

1. Preheat the air fryer to 330°F.
2. Grease two 6-ounce ramekins with butter and then coat it with sugar. Just place a teaspoon of sugar into the ramekins and shake them around until the sugar has coated the butter. Dump out any excess sugar.
3. In a double boiler or microwave, melt the chocolate and butter together until a smooth mixture is created.
4. In a bowl, vigorously beat the egg yolks. Add the vanilla extract and sugar gradually and whisk well again.

5. Add the chocolate-butter mixture into the egg yolk mixture in a gradual manner. Whisk continuously to mix well.
6. Add the flour and combine well so there are no lumps.
7. In another bowl, whisk the egg white until these form soft peaks. Use a hand mixer for faster results.
8. Fold the whipped egg whites into the chocolate mixture. Add the egg whites gradually and use gentle folding motions so that the air doesn't get knocked out, so to speak, from the egg whites.
9. Carefully transfer the final batter into the ramekins but leave a ½-inch space at the top.
10. Place the ramekins into the air fryer and bake the batter for 14 minutes at 330°F.
11. Remove from the air fryer, dust with powdered sugar, and serve with heavy cream on the side. Serve immediately.

S'MORES IN A BANANA TREAT

Preparation Time: 15 minutes | Servings: 4

Nutrition Info (per serving)
Calories: 334 | Fat: 8 g | Protein: 4 g | Carbs: 62 g

INGREDIENTS:

- 4 ripe bananas
- 3 tablespoons graham cracker cereal
- 3 tablespoons peanut butter chips (cut into small chunks, if needed)
- 3 tablespoons semi-sweet chocolate chips (cut into small chunks, if needed)
- 3 tablespoons mini marshmallows

INSTRUCTIONS:

1. Preheat the air fryer to 400°F.
2. Slice the unpeeled bananas lengthwise but don't slice through to the bottom. Slice along the inside of the curve so that when the sliced banana is opened, so to speak, a pocket is created with the peel at the bottom intact.
3. Combine the graham cracker cereal, peanut butter chips, chocolate chips, and marshmallows in a bowl.
4. Place an equal amount of the filling into the pocket of each banana.
5. Place the stuffed bananas into the air fryer basket. Rest them against each other so that these stay upright with the filling facing up.

6. Cook them for 6 minutes at 400°F. Check for doneness, if you want, at the 4-minute mark. The bananas should be soft to the touch while their peels have blackened, and the marshmallows are melted and toasted.
7. Remove from the air fryer, let them cool for 2-3 minutes, and serve on a plate with spoons for getting the filling.

SINGLE SERVE CHOCOLATE MUG CAKE

Preparation Time: 15 minutes | Servings: 1

Nutrition Info (per serving)
Calories: 186 | Fat: 11 g | Protein: 4 g | Carbs: 40 g

INGREDIENTS:

- ¼ cup self-rising flour
- 1 tablespoons cocoa powder
- 1 tablespoon caster sugar
- 3 tablespoons coconut oil
- 3 tablespoons whole milk

INSTRUCTIONS:

1. Mix all the ingredients in an oven-proof mug. Be sure to mix well to ensure a delicious chocolate taste with every spoonful.
2. Place the mug in the air fryer and cook at 392°F for 10 minutes.
3. Serve warm.

Cooking Tip: Use a ramekin instead of a mug in case of space issues. Vary the baking time depending on your preference in texture – 10 minutes is fine for a lava cake, 13 minutes for a cake with a melted chocolate center but not a runny one, and 17 minutes for a more traditional cake.

APPLE FRIES WITH CARAMEL CREAM DIP

Preparation Time: 20 minutes | Servings: 8

Nutrition Info (per serving)
Calories: 135 | Fat: 4 g | Protein: 1 g | Carbs: 30 g

INGREDIENTS:

- 3 apples, preferably Honeycrisp or Pink Lady
- ½ cup flour
- 3 eggs, whisked
- 1 cup graham cracker crumbs (or smash graham crackers in a plastic bag until these are crumbled)
- ¼ cup sugar
- ½ pound cream cheese, whipped
- ¾ cup caramel sauce

INSTRUCTIONS:

1. Preheat the air fryer to 380°F. Be sure to spray the basket with oil.
2. Peel, core and slice the apples into wedges.
3. In a large bowl, toss the flour and apple slices until well-coated.
4. Set up a dredging station – the beaten eggs in a one bowl and the crushed graham crackers and sugar in another bowl.
5. Dip each coated apple slice into the beaten eggs followed by dipping into the graham cracker mixture. Be sure to coat all sides.

APPLE FRIES WITH CARAMEL CREAM DIP

6. Place a cookies sheet on the air fryer basket and arrange the apple slices on top of it.
7. Cook the apple slices for 5 minutes at 380°F.
8. Flip the apple slices to the other side and cook for another 2 minutes at 380°F.
9. Meanwhile, make the caramel dip cream by mixing well the ½ cup of the caramel sauce and whipped cream cheese in a bowl. Drizzle the remaining ¼ cup caramel sauce over the resulting dip.
10. Serve the warm apple fries with the caramel cream dip on the side.

RICOTTA AND LEMON CHEESECAKE

Preparation Time: 25 minutes | Servings: 4

Nutrition Info (per serving)
Calories: 317 | Fat: 21 g | Protein: 6 g | Carbs: 23 g

INGREDIENTS:

- 1 lemon
- 1 ¼ pound ricotta
- ¾ cup sugar
- 3 eggs
- 3 tablespoon cornstarch
- 2 teaspoon vanilla extract

INSTRUCTIONS:

1. Preheat the air fryer to 320°F.
2. In a bowl, combine the ricotta, sugar, and vanilla extract as well as the zest and 1 tablespoon of the lemon juice. Combine well until a homogeneous mixture is made.
3. Add the eggs but one at a time only and mix well.
4. Add the cornstarch, too, and mix well.
5. Pour the mixture into an oven-safe dish that will fit into basket.
6. Cook the mixture for 25 minutes at 320°F.
7. Place the dish on a wire rack and let the cheesecake cool before serving.

MERRY BERRY PAVLOVA

Preparation Time: 20 minutes | Servings: 4

Nutrition Info (per serving)
Calories: 179 | Fat: 2 g | Protein: 1 g | Carbs: 36 g

INGREDIENTS:

- 1 lemon
- 5 eggs, separated (Place the egg yolks and egg whites in two separate bowls)
- 2 teaspoons cornstarch, sieved
- ½ cup super-fine sugar
- ¼ cup raspberries
- ¼ cup strawberries
- ¼ cup black grapes
- 1 ounce blueberries
- ½ tablespoon powdered sugar
- 5/6 cup whipped cream
- Red food coloring

INSTRUCTIONS:

1. Heat the air fryer to 320°F.
2. Get the zest of the lemon and its juice, about 1 teaspoon will be sufficient for the recipe.
3. In a bowl, beat the egg whites until these become stiff.

4. Gradually add the super-fine sugar, cornstarch, red food coloring, and lemon juice into the egg whites. Stop beating when the egg whites have formed shiny and stiff peaks. This is the meringue mixture. Set aside.
5. Place a piece of parchment paper on the air fryer's grill pan.
6. Pour the meringue mixture into the paper and smooth it out to create a flat meringue about 1½ inches thick.
7. Cook the meringue mixture at 212°F for 45 minutes. The preheated air fryer will prevent the meringue from running while the reduced temperature will prevent it from burning.
8. Switch off the air fryer after 45 minutes but leave the meringue inside its cooking chamber for 60 minutes. Remove the meringue afterwards and let it cool in room temperature.
9. In a bowl, mix the assorted fruits. Set aside about a handful for garnish.
10. In another bowl, whip the whipped cream and sugar until stiff.
11. Cut the now-cool meringue in half at the horizontal plane so you will get two sides for a sandwich-like dessert.
12. Spread the whipped cream-sugar mixture into the bottom layer and arrange the mixed fruits on top.
13. Place the upper layer on top.
14. Arrange the remaining fruits on top for garnish.

PINEAPPLE, HONEY AND COCONUT DELIGHT

Preparation Time: 20 minutes | Servings: 4

Nutrition Info (per serving)
Calories: 237 | Fat: 9 g | Protein: 6 g | Carbs: 33 g

INGREDIENTS:

- 1 small pineapple
- 1 tablespoon honey
- ½ tablespoon lime juice
- ½ cup grated coconut
- ¼ quart mango sorbet or mango ice cream

INSTRUCTIONS:

1. Preheat the air fryer to 392°F. Line the bottom of its basket with baking parchment but leave a 1/3 inch empty space at the edge.
2. Peel the pineapple and remove its "eyes" and core. Cut it into 8 sections in a lengthwise manner. Place on a plate and set aside.
3. In a bowl, mix the lime juice and honey until smooth.
4. Brush the pineapple slices with the lime juice-honey mixture.
5. Place the coated pineapple slices in the air fryer basket and sprinkle the grated coconut on top.
6. Cook the pineapple slices at 392°F for 12 minutes. These are cooked when the grated coconut are golden brown in color.
7. Serve the slices with a scoop of mango ice cream or sorbet.

CRÈME BRÛLÉE

Preparation Time: 80 minutes including 20-minute resting time | Servings: 4

Nutrition Info (per serving)
Calories: 476 | Fat: 37 g | Protein: 4 g | Carbs: 34 g

INGREDIENTS:

- 1 cup whipped cream
- 2 vanilla pods
- 1 cup milk
- 10 egg yolks
- 4 ½ tablespoons super-fine sugar
- 6 ½ tablespoons granulated sugar

For the garnish:

- 2 tablespoons super-fine white sugar
- 2 tablespoons brown sugar candy
- Handful of mixed blueberries and redcurrants

INSTRUCTIONS:

1. Cut open the vanilla pods to scrape out its seeds.
2. Pour the milk and cream into a pan. Add both the vanilla pods and seeds to the mixture. This is the milk mixture.
3. Place the pan on a stove set to medium heat and heat the mixture to

nearly boiling and then turn off the heat. Whisk the mixture continuously with a whisk. Set aside to cool down a bit (i.e., warm).
4. In a bowl, mix the white super-fine sugar and granulated sugar (i.e., sugar mixture).
5. Beat the egg yolks with a whisk while gradually adding the sugar mixture. Mix well but don't make it too frothy. This is the egg yolk mixture. Set aside.
6. Pass the still warm milk mixture through a sieve to remove the vanilla pods and seeds.
7. Pour the milk mixture into the egg yolk mixture while constantly stirring. Let it rest for 20 minutes to cool down.
8. Fill ramekin dishes with the final mixture.
9. Cook crème brûlées at 200°F for 45-50 minutes.
10. Let them cool fully in room temperature once cooked.
11. In a blender or food processor, blend the brown sugar candy and super-fine white sugar. This will be the crunchy layer over the crème brûlées – just sprinkle a fine later over each one.
12. Using a portable kitchen blowtorch, melt the sugar layer to form a caramelized layer.
13. Garnish the crème brûlées with fresh fruits, like berries, or with spun sugar.

LEMON BUTTER POUND CAKE

Preparation Time: 40 minutes | Servings: 8

Nutrition Info (per serving)
Calories: 370 | Fat: 21 g | Protein: 5 g | Carbs: 42 g

INGREDIENTS:

- 1 ¼ cups cake flour
- 1 stick butter, softened
- ½ cup muscovado sugar
- 1 large egg
- 1 teaspoon vanilla essence
- 1 teaspoon butter flavoring
- 1 ½ cup milk
- 1 lemon, for zest and juice
- Pinch of salt

For the glaze:

- 1 cup powdered sugar
- 2 tablespoons freshly-squeezed lemon juice

INSTRUCTIONS:

1. Preheat the air fryer to 350°F.

LEMON BUTTER POUND CAKE

2. In a mixing bowl, combine the softened butter and sugar using a hand mixer or table mixer.
3. Fold the egg and beat again.
4. Add the flour, vanilla essence, and butter flavoring as well as a pinch of salt. Mix well so there are little to no lumps.
5. Add the lemon zest and milk. Whisk on low setting until the mixture all the ingredients are incorporated.
6. Grease the air fryer's pan with butter and pour the cake batter into it.
7. Place the pan into the air fryer and bake at 350°F for 15 minutes.
8. Take the pan out of the air fryer and let the cake cool at room temperature for 10-15 minutes.
9. Invert the cake into a serving platter.
10. Make the glaze by mixing the powdered sugar and lemon juice.
11. Drizzle the glaze over the cake and let it sit at room temperatures for 2 hours.

COCONUT BANANA TREAT

Preparation Time: 20 minutes | Servings: 6

Nutrition Info (per serving)
Calories: 198 | Fat: 8 g | Protein: 2 g | Carbs: 23 g

INGREDIENTS:

- 6 ripe bananas, peeled and halved
- ¾ cup breadcrumbs
- 1/3 cup rice flour
- 2 tablespoons coconut oil
- 1 tablespoons coconut sugar
- ¼ teaspoon ground cloves
- ½ teaspoon cinnamon powder
- 1 large egg, beaten

INSTRUCTIONS:

1. In a preheated skillet set over medium heat, place the coconut oil and breadcrumbs for stir frying for about 4 minutes or until the breadcrumbs have a golden brown color. Stir regularly to avoid burning the breadcrumbs.
2. Remove the skillet from the heat and add the cinnamon powder, coconut sugar, and ground cloves. Mix well; this is the breadcrumbs mixture. Transfer to a bowl and set aside.

3. In another bowl, place the rice flour. Coat the sliced bananas with the rice flour; ensure that all sides are well-coated.
4. Dip the coated bananas into a beaten egg followed by rolling them in the breadcrumbs mixture.
5. Bake the bananas in the air fryer at 290°F for 10 minutes.
6. Serve with flaked coconut, if desired.

Cooking Tip: Depending on the capacity of your air fryer, you may have to cook in batches.

HAZELNUT BROWNIE CUPS

Preparation Time: 45 minutes | Servings: 12

Nutrition Info (per serving)
Calories: 334 | Fat: 22 g | Protein: 4 g | Carbs: 32 g

INGREDIENTS:

- ¾ cup semisweet chocolate chips
- 1 stick butter
- ¾ cup all-purpose flour
- ¼ cup muscovado sugar
- ½ cup caster sugar
- 2 large eggs
- ½ teaspoon hazelnut extract
- ¼ cup red wine
- 1 teaspoon pure vanilla extract
- 2 tablespoons cocoa powder
- ½ cup hazelnuts, grounded
- A pinch of salt

INSTRUCTIONS:

1. In a double boiler, melt the butter and chocolate chips together. This is the chocolate mixture.
2. In a mixing bowl, whisk the muscovado sugar, caster sugar, eggs,

HAZELNUT BROWNIE CUPS

hazelnut extract, vanilla extract, and wine until well-incorporated. This is the sugar mixture.
3. Add the chocolate mixture to the sugar mixture. Mix a few times.
4. Add the all-purpose flour, ground hazelnuts, cocoa powder, and a pinch of salt to the chocolate and sugar mixture.
5. Mix everything until a smooth and creamy mixture is created.
6. Line muffin cups with cupcake liners.
7. Pour the batter into the muffin cups and place them into the air fryer.
8. Bake them at 360°F for 30 minutes.

TARTE TATIN

Preparation Time: 45 minutes | Servings: 4

Nutrition Info (per serving)
Calories: 280 | Fat: 8 g | Protein: 0 g | Carbs: 50 g

INGREDIENTS:

- 2 ounces cold butter, sliced thinly
- 1 egg yolk
- ½ cup all-purpose flour
- 1 large baking apple, such as Jonagold or Elstar
- 2 tablespoons sugar

INSTRUCTIONS:

1. Mix half of the butter slices with the egg yolk and all-purpose flour. Blend well to incorporate. Knead to make a smooth ball of dough. Add a few tablespoons of water, if needed.
2. Scatter a handful of flour into a work surface and roll the dough into a round-shaped, 15-centimer-thick top crust for the tarte tatin. Set aside while you make the filling.
3. Preheat the air fryer to 392°F.
4. Peel the apple and remove its core. Slice it into 12 wedges.
5. Place the remaining butter slices into a 15-centimer round fixed-base cake pan. Sprinkle sugar on top of the butter slices.

TARTE TATIN

6. Arrange the 12 apple slices in a circular pattern on top of the butter-sugar base.
7. Cover the apple slices with the dough and press it down along the inside edge of the pan. Trim the edges with a knife, if needed.
8. Place the cake pan on top of the air fryer basket and slide both into the appliance.
9. Bake the tarte tatin at 392°F for 25 minutes or until the tarte tatin's top crust has a golden brown color.
10. Serve warm with vanilla sauce or vanilla ice cream.

BUTTER AND MARSHMALLOW FLUFF TURNOVERS

Preparation Time: 35 minutes | Servings: 4

Nutrition Info (per serving)
Calories: 121 | Fat: 8 g | Protein: 2 g | Carbs: 11 g

INGREDIENTS:

- 4 sheets filo pastry
- 4 tablespoons chunky peanut butter
- 4 teaspoons marshmallow fluff
- 2 ounces butter, melted
- A pinch of sea salt

INSTRUCTIONS:

1. Preheat the air fryer to 360°F.
2. Brush the first sheet filo pastry with the melted butter.
3. Place the second sheet of filo pastry on top of the first. Brush with butter on top, too.
4. Repeat the process until all 4 sheets have been layered and buttered.
5. Cut the layered filo sheets into 4 pieces of 13 x 12" strips. Use a sharp knife for cutting,
6. Place a tablespoon of peanut butter and a tablespoon of marshmallow fluff on each of the filo strips. Place the mixture on the underside only.
7. Fold the tip of the filo strip over the filling so that a triangle is

created. Using a zigzag pattern, repeat the process until the filling is fully covered by the filo strip.
8. Seal the ends with a pat of butter.
9. Place the turnovers into the air fryer basket and bake for 3-5 minutes or until these are puffy and golden brown in appearance.
10. Remove from the basket and place on a plate for serving. Sprinkle with sea salt to get a sweet and salty flavor.

CHERRY CLAFOUTIS

Preparation Time: 30 minutes | Servings: 4

Nutrition Info (per serving)
Calories: 173 | Fat: 2 g | Protein: 6 g | Carbs: 30 g

INGREDIENTS:

- 7/8 cup fresh cherries, pitted (or 1 jar of cherries, drained of its juice)
- 3 tablespoons crème de cassis
- ¼ cup flour
- 1 egg
- 2 tablespoons sugar
- ½ cup sour cream
- 1/3 ounce butter
- A pinch of salt
- Powdered sugar for garnish

INSTRUCTIONS:

1. Preheat the air fryer to 356°F.
2. In a bowl, mix the pitted cherries with the crème de cassis. This is the cherries filling.
3. In another bowl, mix the flour, egg, sugar, sour cream, and a pinch of salt to make a smooth and thick dough. Add a few drops of water for more moisture but don't add more.
4. Grease a 15-centimeter cake pan with butter.

CHERRY CLAFOUTIS

5. Pour the batter into the cake pan, place the cherries filling on top of it, and top with the remaining butter chunks.
6. Place the cake pan into the air fryer basket and slide both into the air fryer's cooking chamber.
7. Bake the cherry clafoutis at 356°F for 25 minutes. It's done when the top has a golden brown color.
8. Remove the cherry clafoutis from the cake pan after cooling it for 5-10 minutes.
9. Sprinkle a generous dusting of powdered sugar on top.
10. Slice and serve warm.

APRICOT AND BLACKBERRY CRUMBLE

Preparation Time: 30 minutes | Servings: 4

Nutrition Info (per serving)
Calories: 232 | Fat: 11 g | Protein: 4 g | Carbs: 34 g

INGREDIENTS:

- 1 cup fresh apricot, pitted and cut into cubes
- 2/3 cup sugar
- ½ cup fresh blackberries
- ½ cup flour
- 1 ¾ ounce cold butter, sliced into cubes
- 1 tablespoon lemon juice
- 1 tablespoon water

INSTRUCTIONS:

1. Preheat the air fryer to 392°F.
2. In a bowl, mix the cubed apricots and blackberries with 2 tablespoons and lemon juice. This is the fruit mix.
3. Grease a round, shallow 16-centimeter cake tin with butter.
4. Spread the fruit mix on the cake tin.
5. In another bowl, make the crumble by mixing the butter, cold water, and remaining sugar. Scrunch the mixture using your fingers so that a crumbly texture is created.

APRICOT AND BLACKBERRY CRUMBLE

6. Spread the crumble over the fruit and press lightly on top.
7. Place the tin on the air fryer basket and into the cooking chamber.
8. Bake the crumble at 392°F for 20 minutes.
9. Serve the crumble any way you desire – hot, lukewarm, or cold. Serve with vanilla sauce, vanilla ice cream, or whipped cream.

PEAR AND APPLE CRISP WITH WALNUTS

Preparation Time: 30 minutes | Servings: 6

Nutrition Info (per serving)
Calories: 343 | Fat: 18 g | Protein: 5 g | Carbs: 43 g

INGREDIENTS:

- ½ pound baking apples, cored and sliced thinly
- ½ pound pears, cored and sliced thinly
- 1 cup all-purpose flour
- 1/3 cup brown sugar
- 1/3 cup muscovado sugar
- 1 tablespoon butter
- 1 teaspoon ground cinnamon
- 1 teaspoon vanilla extract
- ¼ cup walnuts, chopped
- ¼ teaspoon ground cloves
- Whipped cream for garnish

INSTRUCTIONS:

1. Preheat the air fryer at 340°F.
2. Grease lightly a baking dish, which should fit into the air fryer's cooking chamber.
3. Arrange the sliced apples and pears on the bottom of the baking dish.

4. In a mixing bowl, mix the all-purpose flour, brown and muscovado sugar, butter, ground cinnamon, vanilla extract, and ground cloves. The result should be coarse crumbs that will serve as the top layer of the dessert.
5. Spread the coarse crumbs over the fruits and top with the chopped walnuts.
6. Place the baking dish on top of the basket and both into the air fryer.
7. Bake the dessert at 340°F for 20 minutes.
8. Serve the crumble at room temperature with a side of whipped cream.

PEAR PARCELS

Preparation Time: 30 minutes | Servings: 4

Nutrition Info (per serving)
Calories: 199 | Fat: 0 g | Protein: 1 g | Carbs: 48 g

INGREDIENTS:

- 4 sheets puff pastry
- 2 small pears, peeled with the pips removed and then halved
- 2 cups vanilla custard
- 2 tablespoons sugar
- A pinch of cinnamon powder
- 1 large egg, lightly beaten
- Whipped cream and chocolate shavings for garnish

INSTRUCTIONS:

1. Preheat the air fryer to 329°F.
2. In a bowl, combine the sugar and cinnamon powder (i.e., sugar mixture).
3. In each separate sheet of puff pastry, place an equal amount of vanilla custard in the center and place ½ of a pear on top.
4. Coat the sliced pear with the egg (i.e., an egg brush) and sprinkle with the sugar mixture.
5. Fold the edges of the puff pastry to cover the coated pear. Do the rest for the three remaining puff pastry.

6. Place the 4 pear pastries into the air fryer basket.
7. Bake them at 329°F for 15 minutes.
8. Remove the cooked pear parcels from the air fryer basket and let it cool for 5 minutes.
9. Serve warm with whipped cream and chocolate shavings on top, as well as vanilla custard on the side.

CHOCOLATE LAVA CAKE

Preparation Time: 30 minutes | Servings: 4

Nutrition Info (per serving)
Calories: 367 | Fat: 21 g | Protein: 4 g | Carbs: 42 g

INGREDIENTS:

- 1 cup dark cocoa candy melts
- 1 stick butter
- 4 tablespoons super-fine sugar
- 1 tablespoon honey
- 2 large eggs
- 4 tablespoons self-rising flour
- ¼ teaspoon cinnamon powder
- ¼ teaspoon grated nutmeg
- A pinch of ground cloves
- A pinch of salt

INSTRUCTIONS:

1. Preheat the air fryer to 350°F.
2. Get four oven-safe custard cups and spray them with non-stick cooking oil.
3. Place the butter and chocolate candy melts into a microwave-safe bowl. Melt the two ingredients – set the microwave on high for 30-60 seconds. This is the chocolate mixture.

CHOCOLATE LAVA CAKE

4. In a mixing bowl, combine and whish the sugar, honey and eggs until a frothy mix is made. This is the sugar mixture.
5. Add the chocolate mixture to the sugar mixture, and whisk a few times.
6. Add the flour, cinnamon powder, grated nutmeg, ground cloves, and salt into the mixture. Whisk until the ingredients are well-incorporated.
7. Spoon the batter into the custard cups and place them into the air fryer.
8. Bake them at 350°F for 12 minutes.
9. Once cooked, take the custard cups out of the air fryer and let the cake rest for 5 minutes.
10. Flip each cup upside down onto individual small serving plates.
11. Serve with chocolate syrup and fruits, if desired.

TANGY ORANGE CARROT CAKE

Preparation Time: 30 minutes | Servings: 8

Nutrition Info (per serving)
Calories: 245 | Fat: 12 g | Protein: 3 g | Carbs: 31 g

INGREDIENTS:

- 2 large carrots, peeled and grated
- 1 ¾ cup self-rising flour
- ¾ cup brown sugar
- 1 teaspoon mixed spice
- 2 large eggs
- 10 tablespoons olive oil
- 2 cups icing sugar
- 2 tablespoons milk
- 4 tablespoons butter, melted
- 1 large orange, for the zest and juice

INSTRUCTIONS:

1. Preheat the air fryer to 360°F. Line the basket with baking sheet.
2. In a bowl, combine the grated carrots, flour, sugar, and mixed spice. Stir well to combine.
3. Make a crater in the center of the dry ingredients.
4. Add the milk, eggs, and olive oil into the center.
5. Combine the dry and wet ingredients to make a smooth batter.

6. Place the batter into the preheated tin.
7. Bake the batter at 360°F for 5 minutes.
8. Reduce the air fryer temperature to 320°F and bake the cake for 5 minutes more.
9. Make the frosting by combining the orange juice and rind, as well as the icing sugar and butter. Beat the mixture until it's smooth.
10. Let the cake cool at room temperature for 10 minutes.
11. Remove the cake from its tin and place on a serving plate.
12. Top the cake with the frosting before serving.

EASY CHOCOLATE ÉCLAIRS WITH A FLAIR

Preparation Time: 30 minutes | Servings: 4

Nutrition Info (per serving)
Calories: 267 | Fat: 19 g | Protein: 6 g | Carbs: 53 g

INGREDIENTS:

For the éclair dough:

- 1 ¾ ounce butter
- 2/3 cup water
- ½ cup all-purpose flour
- 3 large eggs

For the cream filling:

- 1 teaspoon icing sugar
- 1 teaspoon vanilla essence
- 2/3 cup whipped cream

For the chocolate topping:

- ¼ cup milk chocolate, chopped into small chunks
- ¾ ounce butter
- 1 tablespoon whipped cream

INSTRUCTIONS:

1. Preheat the air fryer to 356°F.

For the éclair dough:

1. In a non-stick pan, place the water and butter. Place the pan over low heat and bring the mixture to a boil.
2. Remove the pan from the heat and stir in the all-purpose flour until well-combined.
3. Return the pan to the stove on low heat. Stir the mixture continuously until a dough forms. Remove from the heat.
4. Transfer the dough to a cold bowl to let it cool down.
5. Add the eggs into the cool dough until a smooth mixture is created.
6. Shape the dough into éclair and place in the air fryer basket.
7. Cook the éclairs in two stages – first, at 356°F for 10 minutes; and second, at 320°F for 8 minutes.
8. Once cooked, remove the éclairs from the air fryers, place on a plate, and set aside to cool for a while.

For the cream filling:

1. In a mixing bowl, whisk the whipped cream, vanilla essence, and icing sugar until a creamy and thick mixture is created.
2. Pour the filling into a piping bag.

For the chocolate topping:

1. In a glass bowl, place the whipped cream, butter, and milk chocolate.
2. Place the glass bowl over a pot of boiling water.
3. Stir the mixture while the ingredients are melting and mixing together. Don't turn off the stove until the mixture has melted well.
4. Pour the smooth mixture into a small bowl. Set aside.

To assemble:

1. Make a hole at the top of each éclair.
2. Pipe the cream filling into the hole using the pastry bag.
3. Dip the cream-filled éclair into the chocolate topping but only dip the top front (i.e., lengthwise).
4. Repeat the process for all the éclairs.
5. Serve warm, perhaps with dark coffee.

SALTY PISTACHIO BROWNIES

Preparation Time: 30 minutes | Servings: 4

Nutrition Info (per serving)
Calories: 183 | Fat: 11 g | Protein: 2 g | Carbs: 24 g

INGREDIENTS:

- ½ cup whole wheat pastry flour
- ½ cup sugar
- ¼ cup cocoa powder
- 1 tablespoon ground flaxseeds
- ¼ teaspoon salt
- ¼ cup non-dairy milk
- ¼ cup aquafaba or the liquid from canned chickpeas
- ½ teaspoon vanilla extract

For the mix-ins ¼ cup of the following:

- Chopped walnuts
- Hazelnuts
- Pecans
- Shredded coconut
- Chocolate chips

INSTRUCTIONS:

1. Preheat the air fryer to 350°F.
2. In one bowl, mix the whole wheat pastry flour, sugar, cocoa powder, ground flaxseeds, and salt.
3. In another bowl, mix the non-dairy milk, aquafaba, and vanilla extract.
4. Add the wet ingredients to the dry ingredients. Mix until well-incorporated.
5. Add the mix-ins with the batter. Mix well again to evenly distribute the mix-ins.
6. Spray non-stick cooking oil on a cake pan or loaf pan, which should fit into the air fryer, or line the pan with parchment paper.
7. Pour the batter into the pan and then into the air fryer basket.
8. Cook the batter at 350°F for 20 minutes. Cook for 5 minutes more in case the cake doesn't pass the knife test. Poke a knife into the middle of the cake – if it comes out clean, then the cake is cooked.

CHOCOLATE BROWNIES WITH CARAMEL SAUCE

Preparation Time: 45 minutes | Servings: 4

Nutrition Info (per serving)
Calories: 311 | Fat: 12 g | Protein: 3 g | Carbs: 50 g

INGREDIENTS:

- ½ cup butter
- ½ cup unsweetened chocolate
- 1 cup self-rising flour
- 1 cup muscovado sugar
- 2 eggs, beaten
- 2 teaspoon pure vanilla extract

For the caramel sauce:

- ½ cup caster sugar
- 2 tablespoons water
- 2/3 cup milk
- ¼ cup butter

INSTRUCTIONS:

1. In a glass bowl, place the butter and chocolate.
2. Place the glass bowl over a pot of boiling water set over a stove on medium heat setting.

CHOCOLATE BROWNIES WITH CARAMEL SAUCE

3. Stir the mixture while the ingredients are melting together.
4. Remove the glass bowl from the pot.
5. Add the flour, eggs, sugar, and vanilla extract into the chocolate mixture. Fold and stir to mix well.
6. Preheat the air fryer to 350°F.
7. Grease a baking dish, which should fit into the air fryer, with butter.
8. Pour the brownie batter into the baking dish and place it into the air fryer.
9. Bake the brownies at 350°F for 15 minutes.
10. Let the baked brownies cool in its baking dish at room temperature.
11. Cut the brownies into squares for serving.
12. Serve with the caramel sauce on top. Add sliced bananas, if desired.

For the caramel sauce:

1. In a small saucepan, mix the water, caster sugar and milk.
2. Place on a stove on medium-low heat.
3. Bring to a boil but stir regularly to make a smooth sauce.
4. Continue cooking even after the mixture has come a boil for about 3 minutes. The mixture should be light brown.
5. Reduce to heat to its lowest setting and continue stirring.
6. After 2 minutes, add the butter gradually until well-incorporated.
7. Remove from heat and let the caramel sauce cool in room temperature.

WHITE CHOCOLATE AND ALMOND COOKIES

Preparation Time: 35 minutes | Servings: 8

Nutrition Info (per serving)
Calories: 318 | Fat: 10 g | Protein: 4 g | Carbs: 21 g

INGREDIENTS:

- 1/3 cup brown sugar
- 7 tablespoons melted butter
- 1 ½ cups self-rising flour
- 2 tablespoons honey
- 2 tablespoons whole milk
- ½ cup white chocolate, melted in double boiler
- 4 tablespoons almonds, chopped

INSTRUCTIONS:

1. Preheat the air fryer to 360°F.
2. In a bowl, whisk the sugar and melted butter. Stop whisking when the mixture has a fluffy texture.
3. Stir the flour, honey, white chocolate, and whole milk into the butter.
4. Add the chopped almonds and mix well again.
5. Shape the cookie dough into your desired shapes and thickness.
6. Place the cookies into the air fryer basket.
7. Bake the cookies at 360°F for 18 minutes.
8. Serve the cookies warm or cool, perhaps with orange juice or coffee.

Made in the USA
Middletown, DE
18 May 2020